Study Guide for
The Western Dream of Civilization:
The Modern World

Volume II

Fifth Edition

Study Guide for
The Western Dream of Civilization:
The Modern World
Volume II

Fifth Edition

Doug Cantrell

Mary A. Rigney

Barbara D. Ripel

Stephen J. Natoli

Abigail Press

Wheaton, IL 60189

Design and Production: Abigail Press
Typesetting: Abigail Press
Typeface: AGaramond
Cover Art: Sam Tolia

Study Guide for
The Western Dream of Civilization:
The Modern World
Volume II

Fifth Edition, 2017
Printed in the United States of America
Translation rights reserved by the publisher
ISBN 1-890919-00-4 13-digit 978-1-890919-00-9

Contents

CHAPTER TWELVE

THE REFORMATION
· ·

IDENTIFICATION: Briefly describe each term.

Protestant Reformation

Martin Luther

Clerical Pluralism

Ninety-five Theses

Great Schism

Babylonian Captivity

Mysticism

Brotherhood of the Eleven Thousand Virgins

Girolamo Savonarola

Brethren of the Common Life

Thomas Kempis

Indulgences

Pope Leo X

Albert of Magdeburg

Frederick of Saxony

Dominican Order

Charles V

Luther's Five Theological Principles

Peasant Revolt

Ulrich von Hutten

Diet of Speyer

Confession of Augsburg

Habsburg-Valois Wars

Peace of Augsburg

John Calvin

Five Principles of Calvinistic Theology

Anabaptists

Henry VIII

Act in Restraint of Appeals

Act for the Submission of Clergy

Supremacy Act

Sir Thomas More

John Fisher

Thomas Cromwell

Mary Tudor

Elizabeth I

Puritans

Elizabethan Settlement

Thirty-nine Articles

John Knox

The Book of Common Order

Mary, Queen of Scots

Catholic Reformation

Roman Inquisition

Council of Trent

Society of Jesus

Philip II

Spanish Armada

Huguenots

St. Bartholomew's Day Massacre

War of the Three Henry's

Thirty Years War

Edict of Nantes

Peace of Westphalia

Sabbats

TRUE/FALSE: Indicate whether each statement is true (T) or false (F). The correct answers are given at the end of the chapter.

1. John Calvin began the Protestant Reformation by posting the Ninety-five _____Theses on the door of Wittenberg Castle Church in 1517.

_____2. The selling of indulgences was one thing that led to the Protestant Reformation.

_____3. The most important event in the lives of sixteenth-century Europeans was overseas exploration.

_____4. The Peasant Revolt began in Swabia in 1535.

_____5. The use of the printing press was important in the spread of the Protestant faith throughout Europe.

_____6. War broke out between German Protestant princes and Charles V in 1546.

_____7. The Diet of Augsburg produced a settlement between Catholics and Protestants in Germany in 1555.

_____8. Ulrich Zwingli introduced the Reformation into Switzerland.

_____9. Martin Luther wrote *Institutes of the Christian Religion* that outlined the Protestant beliefs in 1536.

_____10. Anabaptist was the name given to various left wing sects that embraced the Reformation.

_____11. The English Reformation began when Pope Clement VIII refused to grant Henry VIII an annulment of his marriage to Catherine of Argon.

_____12. John Calvin was the most important Reformation figure in Scotland.

_____13. The term Catholic Reformation and Counter Reformation generally refer to the same thing.

_____14. The Council of Trent met off and on for 35 years.

_____15. Angela Merici founded the Ursuline Order of Nuns.

_____16. Catholics and Protestants both viewed each other as heretics.

_____17. Phillip II of Spain was one of the most fervent anti-Protestant rulers.

_____18. The Spanish Armada contained more ships than the English fleet that defeated it.

_____19. The Thirty Years War killed millions of people from 1618 until 1648.

_____20. The Treaty of Westphalia officially ended the Thirty Years War.

_____21. Men were more likely to be accused of witchcraft than were women.

_____22. Catholics viewed marriage as a legal contract while Protestants viewed it as a holy sacrament that generally could not be dissolved.

_____23. Protestants believed that celibacy was necessary for a minister to lead a religious life.

_____24. Tradition in many European countries held that witches rode broomsticks to meetings with the Devil and other witches called sabbats where they engaged in wild sexual orgies.

_____25. From 900 to 1000 women were probably executed across the European continent for practicing witchcraft.

FILL-IN-THE-BLANKS: Write the appropriate word(s) to complete the sentence. The correct answers are given at the end of the chapter.

1. _____ was a religious confrontation between Catholics and Protestants throughout Europe that lasted for more than a century, produced countless wars, and led to the deaths of thousands of people.

2. _____ was an attempt to give papal authority to church councils and make the papacy a constitutional monarchy.

3. _____ was a Dominican Friar who wanted to outlaw materialism and secularism within the Catholic Church.

4. _____ was a Mystic organization active in Holland. Its members lived simple lives and performed daily acts of charity in an attempt to imitate Christ.

5. _____ was the German Augustinian monk who officially broke with the Catholic Church and launched the Protestant Reformation.

6. _____ was a document written in Latin and sent to Archbishop Albert in which Martin Luther stated his objection to the sale of indulgences.

7. _____ was the Dominican Friar whose selling of indulgences near Wittenberg upset Martin Luther.

8. _____ was the German nobleman who offered Martin Luther protection in Wartburg Castle after Charles V branded the reformer an outlaw.

9. _____ is the Protestant doctrine that holds that after consecration the bread and wine are changed spiritually so that the presence of Christ is found but the wafer and wine are not really transformed into the body and blood.

10. _____, published by Luther in 1525, criticized German nobles and blamed them for causing the peasant revolt.

11. _____ was a meeting held in 1529 that gave rise to the term Protestant in conjunction with the Reformation.

12. _____, written by John Calvin in 1536, discussed Calvin's religious ideas.

13. _____ is the Calvinistic doctrine that holds that God had decided who was damned and who was saved prior to birth.

14. _____ is the type of government John Calvin established in Geneva to govern both the city and his church.

15. _____ was the English monarch who took England out of the Catholic Church.

16. _____, passed by the British Parliament in 1534, required priests and other church officials to obey the king's rules and forbade Christians from publishing theological principles without consent of the monarch.

17. _____, the half-sister of Catherine of Argon, tried to undo the English Reformation during her reign from 1553 to 1558.

18. _____ was the name given to laws enacted during the reign of Elizabeth I that required every English man and woman to attend Anglican services and imposed fines rather than execution on those who refused.

19. _____ was the most important Reformation figure in Scotland.

20. _____, published in 1564, was adopted as the official liturgical tool in the Presbyterian Church.

21. _____ is the term Catholics use to refer to the movement that put the Church's affairs in order after the Protestant Reformation broke out.

22. _____ was the primary strategy Pope Paul III employed to reform the Catholic Church. Its members met off and on from 1545 to 1563.

23. _____ was created by Pope Paul III to fight the spread of Protestantism within Catholic countries.

24. _____ commanded the Spanish army sent by Philip II to crush the Dutch rebellion.

25. _____ was the name given to males believed to practice witchcraft.

MULTIPLE CHOICE: Circle the correct response. The correct answers are given at the end of the chapter.

1. What is generally considered the most monumental event in the lives of sixteenth century Europeans?
   a. The Renaissance
   b. The Reformation
   c. The Discovery of America
   d. The Industrial Revolution

2. Which was not a problem within the Catholic Church that led to the outbreak of the Reformation?
   a. Immorality
   b. Clerical Pluralism
   c. Forbidding the sale of Indulgences
   d. Clerical Ignorance

3. All but one of the following was part of Luther's theology.
   a. Salvation by good deeds
   b. Religious authority resides only in the Bible
   c. The church was the body of Christ
   d. Priesthood of the believer

4. Which one of the following is not associated with the Catholic Reformation?
    a. The Inquisition
    b. The Council of Trent
    c. Establishment of the Jesuit Order
    d. Issuance of the Ninety-five Theses

5. What was the bloodiest of all wars that rocked Europe as a result of the Reformation?
    a. The War of the Three Henrys
    b. The War of the Spanish Succession
    c. The Thirty Years War
    d. The Dutch Revolt

6. What was the law issued by Ferdinand of Styria in 1629 that ordered all property taken from Catholics since 1552 returned.
    a. The Restoration Edict
    b. The Augsburg Law
    c. The Protestant Proclamation
    d. The Law of Transubstantiation

7. What does the idea of predestination hold?
    a. That God chooses who is going to heaven before birth
    b. That individuals can choose whether they are going to heaven or hell
    c. That people who live morally upright lives on earth will go to heaven
    d. That good works are essential to enter heaven

8. What does the idea of consubstantiation hold?
    a. That the presence of Christ is found in the wafer and wine but they are not actually transformed into the body and blood
    b. That during the Eucharist words uttered by the priest miraculously transforms the wafer and wine into the actual body and blood of Christ
    c. That all people are one with God
    d. That all people are one within the grace of Christ

9. Which one of the following was not one of the five principles of Calvin's theology?
    a. Predestination
    b. Total Depravity of Humankind
    c. Unmerited Grace
    d. Unlimited Atonement

10. According to Martin Luther, where did religious authority reside?
    a. In the Bible and in traditional Church teachings
    b. With Priests
    c. Only in the Bible
    d. With the Pope and God

11. According to the best estimates of historians, what was the death toll from the Peasant Rebellion?
    a. Less than 10,000
    b. Greater than 75,000
    c. More than one million
    d. About 350,000

12. What was one of the most important things that attracted rulers and nobles to Lutheranism?
    a. The idea that a person could go to heaven if he or she performed good works
    b. The idea of Priesthood of the Believer
    c. The use of ministers rather than priests
    d. Materialism

13. What gave rise to the use of the term Protestant to describe proponents of the Reformation?
    a. A document produced at the Diet of Speyer in 1529 that protested an order allowing no new religious idea in Germany
    b. A document produced at the Council of Trent criticizing the use of the word "Reformation"
    c. A Catholic attempt to portray Reformers in a negative light
    d. None of the above

14. Who was the Swiss theologian who believed, like Luther, that a personal study of scripture was necessary to lead a Christian life?
    a. John Calvin
    b. Ulrich Zwingli
    c. John Knox
    d. Erasmus

15. Which of the following statements illustrates the primary difference between the theology of Zwingli and Luther?
    a. Luther saw baptism and communion as necessary; Zwingli did not think they were necessary.
    b. Luther believed a personal study of scripture was necessary to lead a Christian life while Zwingli thought it was unnecessary for the individual to study scripture.
    c. Zwingli rejected the use of priests as intermediaries between God and man while Luther allowed priests to serve in this role.
    d. Zwingli allowed ministers to marry while Luther forbade ministers from marrying.

16. Which Protestant Reformer made the statement that people were "as meaningless to God as grains of sand upon the seashore"?
    a. Martin Luther
    b. John Calvin
    c. John Knox
    d. Ulrich Zwingli

17. Which religious group generally rejected infant baptism?
    a. Calvinists
    b. Catholics
    c. Protestants
    d. Anabaptists

18. All but one of the following is characteristic of Anabaptists.
    a. Religious diversity
    b. They did not recognize the church in an institutional form
    c. They allowed priests
    d. Religious tolerance

19. What caused Henry VIII of England to join the Reformation?
    a. He opposed the appointment of Leo X as Pope.
    b. Pope Clement VII refused to grant an annulment of Henry's marriage to his wife Catherine.
    c. Henry got involved in the Habsburg-Valois War in Italy.
    d. Henry wanted to confiscate Catholic land in England.

20. Which one of the following was executed because he or she refused to support the English Reformation?
    a. John Fisher
    b. Sir Walter Raleigh
    c. John Calvin
    d. Elizabeth I

21. Which one of the following was not a result of the Protestant Reformation?
    a. Various religious conflicts erupted throughout Europe.
    b. Establishment of a theocracy in Geneva
    c. The Catholic Church lost vast amounts of land.
    d. The Muslim religion faced serious decline when Protestants began to preach in Islamic countries.

22. Which one of the following was not an achievement of the Council of Trent?
    a. Many abuses within the Catholic Church were corrected.
    b. Protestant positions on Scripture, sacraments, and free will were accepted.
    c. All seven sacraments are valid representations of God's grace.
    d. Priest were the only people authorized to administer the sacraments.

23. What was the order issued by Henry IV in 1598 that allowed Huguenots to legally hold worship services and exist as a religious minority throughout France?
    a. Edict of Nantes
    b. Peace of Augsburg
    c. The Holy Writ
    d. Institutes of the Christian Faith

24. Why did the Thirty Years War last so long?
    a. No ruler had the ability and resources to win a complete victory.
    b. God intervened on the side of the Protestants.
    c. Muslim armies came to Germany to help the Catholics.
    d. Elizabeth I of England sent an army to help the Catholics.

25. How did Protestant writers generally justify the verbal and physical abuse women suffered?
    a. As justified because women were not as physically strong as men
    b. As justified because women were not as smart as men
    c. As justified as punishment for sins committed by the Biblical Eve
    d. As justified because women were more apt to be morally corrupted by Catholic teaching

MATCHING: Match the response in column A with the item in column B.

Column A

a. Martin Luther
b. John Calvin
c. Protestant Reformation
d. Indulgences
e. Clerical pluralism
f. Brotherhood of the Eleven Thousand Virgins
g. Philip Melanchthon
h. *The Babylonian Captivity*
i. Priesthood of the Believer
j. Ulrich von Hutten
k. Ulrich Zwingli
l. Charles V
m. Peace of Augsburg
n. The Elect
o. Geneva
p. Anabaptists
q. Eschatology
r. Melchiorites
s. Pope Julius II
t. Act in Restraint of Appeals
u. Sir Thomas More
v. Elizabeth I
w. Thirty-nine Articles
x. Ignatius Loyola
y. Battle of Lepanto

Column B

_____ 1. Founded the Jesuit Order in 1540.
_____ 2. Began the Protestant Reformation when he nailed the Ninety-five Theses to the door of Wittenberg Castle Church.
_____ 3. Executed because he opposed the English Reformation.
_____ 4. The term used by Calvinists to refer to people they believed were "saved."
_____ 5. The second most important figure in the Protestant Reformation.
_____ 6. One of the most successful rulers England ever had.
_____ 7. The most momentous event in the lives of sixteenth century Europeans.
_____ 8. A term that generally refers to more radical Protestant groups that were part of the Reformation.
_____ 9. The practice of holding several church benefices or offices simultaneously.
_____ 10. A practice within the Catholic Church by which a person could purchase forgiveness for sins without undergoing repentance.
_____ 11. A belief in the imminent coming of Christ.
_____ 12. A disciple of Luther who claimed that on All Hallow's Eve in 1517 Martin Luther nailed the Ninety-five Theses to the door of Wittenberg Castle Church.
_____ 13. A Holy Roman Emperor who opposed the Protestant Reformation.
_____ 14. An Anabaptist sect that was violently suppressed at Munster.
_____ 15. Gave Henry VIII a special dispensation that allowed him to wed Catherine of Argon, who had been married to Henry's brother Arthur.

_____ 16. A large Mystic organization in Germany.

_____ 17. The city where John Calvin fled after facing trouble in France.

_____ 18. The period from 1309 to 1376 when Philip the Fair forced the Pope to live in Avignon, France.

_____ 19. A celebrated German Humanist who joined Luther in advancing the Reformation.

_____ 20. An agreement in 1555 by which each German prince could determine what religion his kingdom could follow.

_____ 21. A humanist who brought the Reformation to Switzerland.

_____ 22. The idea that individuals can understand God's will as revealed in the Bible through prayer without the aid of priests.

_____ 23. Legalized the English Reformation by forbidding church officials to submit legal appeals to the Roman Pope. Instead, English religious disputes were settled by the English monarch.

_____ 24. A document approved by English bishops in 1563 that briefly outlined Anglican beliefs.

_____ 25. A naval victory that curtailed Islamic power in the Mediterranean.

ESSAY QUESTIONS: (Answer on separate paper)

1. Compare and contrast the theology of Martin Luther and John Calvin.

2. Identify and discuss problems in the Catholic Church that led to the Reformation.

3. Compare the English Reformation to the German Reformation.

4. Discuss why someone would make the following quotation in light of the Protestant Reformation: "More people have been killed in the name of God than for any other reason."

5. How did the Protestant Reformation change the role of women in European society?

ANSWERS TO CHAPTER TWELVE
TRUE/FALSE:

1-F; 2-T; 3-F; 4-F; 5-T; 6-T; 7-T; 8-T; 9-F; 10-T; 11-F; 12-F; 13-T; 14-F; 15-T; 16-T; 17-T; 18-F; 19-T; 20-F; 21-F; 22-F; 23-F; 24-T; 25-F

FILL-IN-THE-BLANKS:

1. Protestant Reformation 2. Concilian Movement 3. Girolamo Savonarola 4. Brethren of the Common Life 5. Martin Luther 6. Ninety-five Theses 7. John Tetzel 8. Duke Frederick III of Saxony 9. Consubstantiation 10. An Admonition to Peace 11. Diet of Speyer 12. *Institutes of the Christian Religion* 13. Predestination 14. Theocracy 15. Henry VIII 16. Act for the Submission of Clergy 17. Mary Tudor 18. Elizabethan Settlement 19. John Knox 20. *Book of Common Order* 21. Catholic Revival or Catholic Reformation 22. Council of Trent 23. The Inquisition 24. Duke of Alva 25. Warlock

MULTIPLE CHOICE:

1-b; 2-c; 3-a; 4-d; 5-c; 6-a; 7-a; 8-b; 9-d; 10-c; 11-b; 12-d; 13-a; 14-b; 15-a; 16-b; 17-d; 18-c; 19-c; 20-a; 21-d; 22-b; 23-a; 24-a; 25-c

MATCHING:
1-x; 2-a; 3-u; 4-n; 5-b; 6-v; 7-c; 8-p; 9-e; 10-d; 11-q; 12-g; 13-l; 14-r; 15-s; 16-f; 17-o; 18-h; 19-j; 20-m; 21-k; 22-i; 23-t; 24-w; 25-y

CHAPTER THIRTEEN

EUROPE IN THE AGE OF ABSOLUTISM

. . . .

IDENTIFICATION: Briefly describe each term.

Sun King

Absolutism

Constitutionalism

Palace of Versailles

Huguenots

Henry of Guise

Duke of Sully

Cardinal Richelieu

Louis XIII

Louis XIV

Jules Mazarin

the Fronde

Jansenists

Jean Baptiste Colbert

L'etat, c'est moi"

un roi, une loi, une foi

War of Three Henrys

Philip III

Philip IV

Saint Bartholomew's Day Massacre

Rudolf of the House of Habsburg

Henry of Navarre/Henry IV

Leopold I

"The Great Elector"

House of Hohenzollern

Edict of Nantes

beard tax

soul tax

Frederick I

Boris Godunov

The Time of Troubles

Michael Romanov

Sophia

Peter I/Peter the Great

Ivan V

James VI/James I

Charles V/Charles I

Guy Fawkes

Great Embassy

The Long Parliament

Cavaliers

Roundheads

the English Civil War

Oliver Cromwell

Rump Parliament

Restoration

the New Model Army

"Merry Monarch"

Charles II

William of Orange

Glorious Revolution

Act of Union (1707)

TRUE/FALSE: Indicate whether each statement is true (T) or false (F). The correct answers are given at the end of the chapter.

_____ 1. The boyars were the lower class in Russia.

_____ 2. Spain's ruling family in the seventeenth century was the House of Hohenzollern.

_____ 3. The King James Bible was first published during the reign of James I.

_____ 4. The first Romanov czar was Michael.

_____ 5. The Thirty Years War ended with the Treaty of Westphalia.

_____ 6. Louis XIV's mother was Marie de Medici.

_____ 7. England had a constitution in the seventeenth century.

_____ 8. One of the House of Bourbon's most powerful rulers was Louis XIV.

_____ 9. French Protestants are Huguenots

_____ 10. The Saint Bartholomew's Day Massacre was caused by tension between Catholics and Muslims.

_____ 11. The "Great Westernizer" was from Austria.

_____ 12. The Gunpowder Plot resulted in the destruction of the British Parliament's meeting house.

_____ 13. Henry of Navarre became the first Bourbon king of France.

_____ 14. Boris Godunov became Czar of Russia after Fedor died.

_____ 15. Sophia was Peter the Great's mother, and she ruled as regent for a time.

_____ 16. "Old Believers" had split from the Anglican Church to protest reforms made by the leaders.

_____ 17. At the end of the Thirty Years War, Brandenburg was considered to be the strongest Protestant state in Germany.

_____ 18. Frederick William I worked hard to create a decentralized government.

_____ 19. Philip II of Spain was a believer in the divine right of kings.

_____ 20. The Spanish Armada was defeated by the English in 1588.

_____ 21. The War of Spanish Succession ended when Philip V became King of Spain.

_____ 22. The War of the Devolution was an attempt by Spain to gain control of the region known today as Belgium.

_____ 23. The Glorious Revolution took place in England.

_____ 24. Louis XIV ultimately inhibited freedom of religion for both Catholics and Protestants in France.

_____ 25. The Fronde was an uprising of peasants who were angered at the cost of food in France.

FILL-IN-THE-BLANKS: Write the appropriate word(s) to complete the sentence. The correct answers are given at the end of the chapter.

1. _____ combined with _____ to make the country of Spain.

2. The word _fronde_ means _____.

3. Cardinal Richelieu's successor was _____.

4. _____ created the Holy Synod in Russia.

5. _____ had seven of his eight great grandparents descended from Joanna "the mad."

6. From 1643-1661 who was the most powerful man in French government? _____.

7. The Church of England is also known as _____.

8. In the _____of 1605 Catholic extremists conspired to kill the king, his ministers, and parliament in an attempt to gain more control over the government of England.

9. King James II was replaced by _____ and _____ in the Glorious Revolution.

10. After Oliver Cromwell removed the members of Parliament that disagreed with him, those who remained were referred to as the _____.

11. _____ liked to be called the *Sun King*.

12. Henry III of France was killed by _____, a Catholic extremist.

13. _____ wrote the *Basilikon Doron*.

14. Ivan the Terrible's son and successor was _____.

15. The _____ formally unified England and Scotland, creating the Kingdom of Great Britain in 1707.

16. Who was known as "The Great Elector"? _____

17. Anne of Austria's father was _____.

18. The supporters of the king during the English Civil War were nicknamed _____.

19.The supporters of Parliament during the English Civil War were nicknamed _____.

20. Charles II of England was sometimes called _____ because he enjoyed the theater, music, and having fun. His reign was a marked change from Cromwell's military dictatorship.

21. The last Tudor monarch in England was _____.

22. How were Mary Stuart and Elizabeth I related? _____

23. The Austrian Habsburgs were generally of what religious faith?_____

24. Leopold I helped form the _____, an alliance among several German states, and other countries including Sweden and Spain.

25. During the English Civil War, Parliament created an army called _____.

MULTIPLE CHOICE: Circle the correct response. The correct answers are given at the end of the chapter.

1. Which monarch brought the British Isles under the rule of one monarch for the first time?
    a. Anne I
    b. Elizabeth I
    c. Charles I
    d. James I

2. The Lord Protector of England after the English Civil War was
    a. Charles Stuart
    b. Oliver Cromwell
    c. Richard Cromwell
    d James Stuart

3. Which of the following did Peter the Great NOT learn during his Great Embassy?
    a. shipbuilding
    b. ceramics
    c. gunnery
    d. engineering

4. Who (probably) said "Paris is well worth a mass?"
    a. Henry III
    b. Henry IV
    c. Henry of Guise
    d. Duke of Sully

5. Who was the last Spanish Habsburg?
   a. Leopold I
   b. Philip IV
   c. Charles II
   d. Matthias

6. The Valois monarchy in France was replaced by
   a. the Stuarts
   b. the Bourbons
   c. the Navarres
   d. the Hohenzollerns

7. The Time of Troubles began with the death of
   a. Ivan the Terrible
   b. Fedor I
   c. Michael Romanov
   d. Boris Godunov

8. Which Spanish king sent the Armada to England?
   a. Philip I
   b. Charles II
   c. Philip II
   d. Charles I

9. Who issued the Edict of Nantes (1598)?
   a. Louis XIII
   b. Louis XIV
   c. Henry III
   d. Henry IV

10. _____ introduced the *Paulette* tax in France.
    a. Henry IV
    b. Duke of Sully
    c. Duke of Monmouth
    d. Henry III

11. Louis XIV's finance minister was
    a. Duke of Sully
    b. Concino Concini
    c. Jean Baptiste Colbert
    d. Cardinal Mazarin

12. Who was executed as a result of the English Civil War?
    a. Oliver Cromwell
    b. Charles I
    c. Richard Cromwell
    d. Charles II

13. Which country is not a part of Great Britain?
    a. England
    b. Ireland
    c. Scotland
    d. Wales

14. Boris Godunov's sister was
    a. Sophia
    b. Irene
    c. Marie de'Medici
    d. Anne of Austria

15. The Time of Troubles happened in
    a. Great Britain
    b. Russia
    c. France
    d. Germany

16. The Act of Settlement settled what exactly?
    a. there would never be another Protestant monarch of France
    b. there would never be another Catholic monarch of France
    c. there would never be another Protestant monarch of England
    d. there would never be another Catholic monarch of England

17. The first Test Act in 1673 did NOT do which of the following
    a. barred non Anglicans from voting
    b. barred non Catholics from voting
    c. barred non Anglicans from holding military office
    d. barred non Anglicans from having the right to assembly

18. The Glorious Revolution was "glorious" because
    a. there was little bloodshed
    b. it restored a Protestant ruler to England
    c. both of the above
    d. neither of the above

19. The first in the line of Austrian Habsburgs was
    a. Leopold I
    b. Ferdinand
    c. Rudolf
    d. Charles II

20. Anne of Austria's father was
    a. Charles I
    b. Louis XIII
    c. Philip III
    d. Rudolf I

21. Which country embraced constitutionalism instead of absolutism?
    a. Great Britain
    b. France
    c. Prussia
    d. Spain

22. Cardinal Mazarin was a citizen of
    a. Germany
    b. France
    c. Italy
    d. Spain

23. The Oprichnik was
    a. the czar's secret police
    b. a secret society in Paris
    c. a socialist newspaper
    d. the Russian military

24. During Sophia's government which group did Russia engage in war?
    a. Germans
    b. Spanish
    c. French
    d. Turks

25. Who was Louis XIII's mother?
    a. Sophia
    b. Marie de Medici
    c. Anne of Austria
    d. Mary Tudor

MATCHING: Match the person with the appropriate country. Countries can used more than once.

_____ 1. Louis XIII	a. Great Britain
_____ 2. Philip III	b. France
_____ 3. Elizabeth I	c. Prussia/Holy Roman Empire
_____ 4. Boris Godunov	d. Russia
_____ 5. Charles II, the Merry Monarch	e. Austria
_____ 6. Henry IV	f. Spain
_____ 7. James II	
_____ 8. Frederick William I	
_____ 9. Peter the Great	
_____ 10. Rudolf	
_____ 11. William and Mary	
_____ 12. Michael Romanov	
_____ 13. Sophia	
_____ 14. Charles II, the Bewitched	
_____ 15. Oliver Cromwell	
_____ 16. Richelieu	
_____ 17. Count of Olivares	

Match each item in Column A with the most appropriate item in Column B

Column A

_____ 18. Rump Parliament

_____ 19. War of Spanish Succession

_____ 20. "devolution"

_____ 21. Jansenists

_____ 22. streltsy

_____ 23. Great Westernizer

_____ 24. boyar

_____ 25. Kirk

Column B (there will be one extra answer)

a. predestination

b. Peter the Great

c. Russian noble

d. daughters of a first marriage favored over any sons born into later unions

e. Russian guardsmen

f. Basilikon Doron

g. remained after Cromwell removed those who opposed him

h. Scottish church

i. Treaty of Utrecht

ESSAY QUESTIONS: (Answer on separate paper)

1. Discuss the Fronde. What effect did it have on Louis XIV's reign?

2. Discuss the rise of Peter the Great in Russia.

3. Discuss the Glorious Revolution in Great Britain.

4. Discuss the English Civil War. Include the main causes and results.

5. Based on your understanding of the subject, give some advantages and disadvantages of having absolutist rule in a country.

ANSWERS TO CHAPTER THIRTEEN

TRUE/FALSE:

1-F; 2-F; 3-T; 4-T; 5-T; 6-F; 7-T; 8-T; 9-T; 10-F; 11-F; 12-F; 13-T; 14-T; 15-F; 16-F; 17-T; 18-F; 19-T; 20-T; 21-T; 22-F; 23-T; 24-T; 25-F

FILL-IN-THE-BLANKS:

1. Castile and Aragon 2. slingshot 3. Mazarin 4. Peter the Great 5. Charles II - Spain
6. Mazarin 7. Anglican 8. Gunpowder Plot 9. William and Mary 10. Rump Parliament
11. Louis XIV 12. Jacques Clement 13. James I 14. Fedor 15. Act of Union
16. Frederick William 17. Philip III 18. Cavaliers 19. Roundheads 20. the Merry Monarch
21. Elizabeth I 22. cousins 23. Catholic 24. League of Augsburg 25. New Model Army

MULTIPLE CHOICE:

1-d; 2-b; 3-b; 4-b; 5-c; 6-b; 7-b; 8-c; 9-d; 10-b; 11-c; 12-b; 13-b; 14-b; 15-b; 16-d; 17-b; 18-c; 19-b; 20-c; 21-a; 22-b; 23-a; 24-d; 25-c

MATCHING:

1-b; 2-f; 3-a; 4-d; 5-a; 6-b; 7-a; 8-c; 9-d; 10-e; 11-a; 12-d; 13-d; 14-f; 15-a; 16-b; 17-f; 18-g; 19-i; 20-d; 21-a; 22-e; 23-b; 24-c; 25-h

CHAPTER FOURTEEN

A NEW KIND OF WORLD

· ·

IDENTIFICATION: Briefly describe each term.

The Great Chain of Being

epistemological transformation

Roger Bacon

Francis Bacon

deductive reasoning

inductive reasoning

Nicholas Copernicus

On the Revolution of Heavenly Spheres

Johannes Kepler

Plato's concept of the Forms

Pope Urban VIII

Galileo Galilei

Natural Law

Isaac Newton

The Principles of Natural Philosophy

William Harvey

Circulation of the Blood

Cartesian geometry

bourgeoisie

commonwealth

The Leviathan

Thomas Hobbes

Essay on Human Understanding

Treatises Concerning Government

John Locke

Oxford University

Whigs

Tories

Alexander Pope

Gulliver's Travels

A Modest Proposal

Francois Marie Arouet

Candide

Denis Diderot

Confessions

Jean Jacques Rousseau

Social Contract

The Burning Times

philosophes

On Crimes and Punishments

On the Wealth of Nations

Immanuel Kant

David Hume

Deism

Baroque

Oratorians

George Frederick Handel

Bernini's *David*

the salon

Seven Years War

TRUE/FALSE: Indicate whether each statement is true (T) or false (F). The correct answers are given at the end of the chapter.

_____ 1. The Scientific Revolution was firmly rooted in European History.

_____ 2. The Roman Catholic Church supported the Scientific Revolution.

_____ 3. Columbus immediately realized he had discovered a new continent.

_____ 4. Historians agree that Galileo started the Scientific Revolution.

_____ 5. Francis Bacon believed science was best studied from the particular to the general.

_____ 6. Only a few famous men were involved in the Scientific Revolution.

_____ 7. One of the chief Arabic contributions to the Western Scientific Revolution was the use of Arabic numerals.

_____ 8. When the Churchmen read Galileo's work they changed their view of the universe to agree with Copernicus and Galileo.

_____ 9. On behalf of science and the people, the Church encouraged the practice of dissecting human bodies.

_____ 10. William Harvey discovered that the heart pumped blood through the body.

_____ 11. The Scientific Revolution was a broad based phenomena which involved all of European society.

_____ 12. Education was a key to opening doors for the middle class.

_____ 13. John Locke's famous theory about human character is called "tabula rasa."

_____ 14. John Locke believed that rulers came to power through the appointment by God, or the theory of divine right.

_____ 15. King William and Queen Mary took the throne of England when they were asked to do so by the English Parliament.

_____ 16. Newspapers and pamphlets were not important during the English political debates.

_____ 17. Many English writers took old Roman names to hide their identities but to justify their ideas.

_____ 18. Paris welcomed Voltaire as its sage and most famous writer.

_____ 19. The notion of witchcraft was defeated by the ideas of the Enlightenment.

_____ 20. A new theory about social dissidents who could be "retrained" into good citizens was the idea of Cesare Beccaria.

_____ 21. "Laissez faire" advocates the idea of free trade.

_____ 22. Adam Smith said that both people and nations operated on the notion of self interest.

_____ 23. David Hume believed that one thing caused another and that all things are connected.

_____ 24. All Enlightenment intellectuals were convinced that the Christian God directed the universe and was directly involved in human life.

_____ 25. Although politics changed during the English and Scientific Revolutions, art forms remained the same as in the Renaissance.

FILL-IN-THE-BLANKS: Write the appropriate word(s) to complete the sentence. The correct answers are given at the end of the chapter.

1. Most scientific ideas before the Scientific Revolution were defined by _____.

2. _____ designed a flying machine to be used in wars.

3. The new western continents were named by _____.

4. John Calvin's concept of Christianity related man to God by a series of _____.

5. The word chemistry is from the language of the _____.

6. Galileo proved Copernicus' theory by using a _____.

7. An interesting fact about Newton's scientific work was that it was the last treatise written in the language of _____.

8. A famous saying of Rene DesCartes was "I think, _____.

9. The Civil War in England ended with the death of _____.

10. Popular literature in England during the 16th and 17th centuries made _____ the strongest part of the government.

11. Voltaire's writings glorified the _____.

12. Jean Jacques Rousseau wrote _____ about the way society was formed in the state of nature.

13. The "Burning Times" refers to a period of _____.

14. Immanuel Kant believed that humans _____.

15. George Frederick Handel wrote his oratories in _____.

16. Musical "plays" were called _____.

17. Many of Rembrant's paintings were done for _____.

18. Bernini's *David*, as compared to Michelangelo's is _____.

19. Baroque art glorifies _____.

20. The salon in France helped women _____.

21. During the Enlightenment, _____ became the language of educated Europeans.

22. Nationalism became a concept particularly associated with the _____ European states.

23. Frederick of Prussia believed women were _____.

24. One of the most prolific music composers of the period was _____.

25. In the theory of Natural Law, even _____ had to conform to the rules.

MULTIPLE CHOICE: Circle the correct response. The correct answers are given at the end of the chapter.

1. Influences in the Enlightenment included all but
    a. the Renaissance
    b. the Reformation
    c. the Roman Republic
    d. the Scientific Revolution

2. The fifteenth century rediscovered notions of
    a. the Greeks
    b. the Romans
    c. the Pietists
    d. the Modernists

3. The Scientific Revolution
    a. reoriented the thought of Western Civilization
    b. was led by the priests
    c. started in the countryside and moved to the cities
    d. was centered in Church policy

4. Columbus' discovery of the New World
    a. was immediately revealed to the European masses
    b. was praised by Prince Henry of Portugal
    c. did not interest most people
    d. would eventually change the European concept of the world

5. One of Luther's favorite phrases was
    a. indulgences are good
    b. communion of saints
    c. the devil made me do it
    d. suffering is required

6. Christian Europe learned much scientific knowledge from
   a. the Russians
   b. the Mongols
   c. the Americans
   d. the Arabs

7. Nicholas Copernicus developed a theory that
   a. humans were born with no personality
   b. the planets, including the Earth, circled the sun
   c. the planets and sun circled the Earth
   d. God was irrelevant to human life

8. Isaac Newton discussed
   a. geography
   b. printing
   c. the idea of natural law
   d. photography

9. Versalius is known for his contributions to
   a. astronomy
   b. medicine
   c. anatomy
   d. mathematics

10. During the seventeenth century, political changes in England
    a. produced new theories of government
    b. made the king supreme
    c. reduced the power of Parliament
    d. said that no woman should rule England

11. Hobbes' *Leviathan*
    a. supported divine right monarchy
    b. talked about human rights
    c. wanted Parliamentary rule
    d. said man was basically good

12. Locke theorized that human beings had
    a. no right to participate in government
    b. no right to own property
    c. had certain rights given by God
    d. were ignorant of natural law

13. The Whigs in England favored
    a. a strong king
    b. high taxes
    c. a dominant role for Parliament
    d. long artificial hair

14. Rousseau's treatise on education was called
    a. "Teach the Young"
    b. "Ideas for the Student"
    c. "Emile"
    d. "The Wisdom of Generations"

15. The *Encyclopedia* was a
    a. collection of stories
    b. collection of the world's knowledge
    c. pieces of advice from learned men
    d. ideas of the philosophes

16. The idea that the history of the world was a process of progress is credited to
    a. John Locke
    b. Isaac Newton
    c. George Louis Buffon
    d. Thomas Jefferson

17. A new religious perspective of the Enlightenment period was called
    a. Papism
    b. Geoism
    c. Deism
    d. Orthodoxy

18. A new style of music in the mid-sixteenth and seventeenth centuries except
    a. operas
    b. cantatas
    c. fugues
    d. tenebrism

19. A transition in music during the sixteenth century was
    a. the use of banjos
    b. the use of the vernacular
    c. no singing parts
    d. audience participation

20. The introduction of complex music with a variety of instruments and voices was called
    a. polyphonic
    b. chaos music
    c. atonal music
    d. pop rock

21. A famous woman painter of the period was
    a. Lucrezia Borgia
    b. Joan of Arc
    c. Artemisa Gentileschi
    d. Eleanor of Acquitaine

22. A connection between art and science is in the
    a. paintings of Titian's students
    b. Tycho Brahe's tables
    c. Johannes Kepler's experiments
    d. There was no connection between art and science.

23. A hallmark of the Restoration in England was
    a. he new king's fancy wardrobe
    b. the opening of the theatres
    c. lending money at interest
    d. joint bank accounts for married couples

24. Education for women in Europe during the sixteenth and seventeenth centuries was
    a. widespread
    b. taught the duties of wife and mother
    c. taught poetry and dancing
    d. was minimal and restricted to the upper class

25. Although called an Enlightened Despot, Frederick of Prussia
    a. wrote literary pieces
    b. believed the people could not rule
    c. wanted to build cities like Paris
    d. wanted to resign his title and live as a farmer

MATCHING: Match the response in column B with the item in column A.
Column A

Column A	Column B
_____ 1. Martin Luther	A. Sun King
_____ 2. Anton van Leeuwenhoek	B. Tabula Rasa
_____ 3. Voltaire	C. Frederick of Prussia
_____ 4. Copernican Theory	D. King's Men
_____ 5. Thomas Hobbes	E. Candide
_____ 6. Partition of Poland	F. anatomical drawings
_____ 7. Venice	G. *Leviathan*
_____ 8. John Locke	H. To Know
_____ 9. Scientific Revolution	I. Fugue
_____ 10. David Hume	J. "cogito ergo sum"
_____ 11. Louis XIV	K. converted to marry
_____ 12. Copernicus	L. a division of mathematics
_____ 13. Galileo	M. to understand nature's laws
_____ 14. Jonathan Swift	N. son of a musician
_____ 15. Francis Bacon	O. Polish mathematician
_____ 16. Tycho Brahe	P. resigned from politics for science
_____ 17. Tories	Q. Successor the Elizabeth I
_____ 18. Versallius	R. microscope
_____ 19. Catherine the Great	S. communion of saints
_____ 20. music	T. against the notion of causality
_____ 21. scio	U. home of Galileo
_____ 22. DesCartes	V. Danish astronomer
_____ 23. Roger Bacon	W. planets circle the sun
_____ 24. Johannes Sebastian Bach	X. *Gulliver's Travels*
_____ 25. James VI	Y. 13th century scientist

ESSAY QUESTIONS: (Answer on separate paper)

1. Why did Copernicus delay the publication of his theories?

2. "The Scientific Revolution of the sixteenth and seventeenth centuries was an epistemological transformation." Discuss this statement.

3. How was art (painting, sculpture, architecture, and music) affected by the Scientific Revolution and the Enlightenment?

4. Why does the text describe the witchcraft craze as a reaction to other events in the sixteenth and seventeenth centuries?

5. How did the ancient Greeks contribute to the Scientific Revolution?

6. Describe John Locke's thesis about the way people learn.

ANSWERS TO CHAPTER FOURTEEN

TRUE/FALSE:

1-T; 2-F; 3-F; 4-F; 5-T; 6-F; 7-T; 8-F; 9-F; 10-T; 11-F; 12-T; 13-T; 14-F; 15-T; 16-F; 17-T; 18-F; 19-F; 20-T; 21-T; 22-T; 23-F; 24-F; 25-F

FILL-IN-THE-BLANKS:

1. the Church; 2. Albrecht Durer; 3. a nameless printer; 4. contracts; 5. Arabic; 6. telescope; 7. Latin; 8. "therefore I am." 9. the king, Charles I; 10. Parliament; 11. individual; 12. Social Contract; 13. witch hunts; 14. had an innate sense of right and wrong; 15. English; 16. operas; 17. town fathers; 18. active and angry; 19. complexity; 20. lead untraditional lives; 21. French; 22. western; 23 inferior and should not rule; 24. Vivaldi; 25. God

MULTIPLE CHOICE:

1-c; 2-a; 3-a; 4-d; 5-b; 6-d; 7-b; 8-c; 9-c; 10-a; 11-a; 12-c; 13-c; 14-c; 15-b; 16-c; 17-c; 18-c; 19-b; 20-a; 21-c; 22-a; 23-b; 24-d; 25-b

MATCHING:

1-S; 2-R; 3-E; 4-W; 5-G; 6-C; 7-U; 8-B; 9-M; 10-T; 11-A; 12-0; 13-N; 14-X; 15-P; 16-V; 17-D; 18-F; 19-K; 20-L; 21-H; 22-J; 23-Y; 24-I; 25-Q

CHAPTER FIFTEEN

THE FRENCH REVOLUTION AND NAPOLEON BONAPARTE, 1789-1815

IDENTIFICATION: Briefly describe each term.

Louis XVI

Napoleon Bonaparte

French Revolution

Marie Antoinette

Assembly of Notables

Estates General

First Estate

Second Estate

Third Estate

Nobles of the Sword

Nobles of the Robe

National Assembly

Bastille

Marquis de Lafayette

Declaration of the Rights of Man and Citizen

The Rights of Women

Mary Wollstonecraft

1791 Constitution

Active citizens

Passive citizens

Civil Constitution of the Clergy

Refactory Priests

Jacobins

September Massacres

Maximilien Robespierre

Edmund Burke

Reign of Terror

Committee of Public Safety

Society of Revolutionary Republican Women

Vendemiaire Massacre

Treaty of Basel

Council of Ancients

Council of Five Hundred

The Directory

Conspiracy of Equals

Constitution of the Year VIII

Code Napoleon

Treaty of Amiens

Battle of Austerlitz

Treaty of Tilsat

Berlin Decree

Continental System

Orders of Council

Peninsular Campaign

Battle of the Nations

Waterloo

TRUE/FALSE: Indicate whether each statement is true (T) or false (F). The correct answers are given at the end of the chapter.

_____1. The execution of Louis XVI caused the French Revolution.

_____2. Bankers were members of the First Estate.

_____3. Church officials were members of the Second Estate.

_____4. The Tennis Court Oath was a pledge by members of the National Assembly not to adjourn until France became a Republic.

_____5. The Declaration of the Rights of Man and Citizen was modeled on the United States Bill of Rights.

_____6. Women were given complete equality with men as part of the French Revolution.

_____7. The 1791 Constitution decentralized the French government.

_____8. Only active citizens could vote under the 1791 Constitution.

_____9. Jacobins represented the majority during the French Revolution.

_____10. The 1791 constitution empowered the poor.

_____11. Numerous "enemies of the state" were executed during the Reign of Terror.

_____12. The Committee of Public Safety instituted a levee en masse.

_____13. An attempt was made during the Reign of Terror to de-Christianize France.

_____14. The Constitution of 1793 was fully implemented in France.

_____15. The White Terror was part of the Reign of Terror.

_____16. Royalists were Frenchmen who wanted to restore the monarchy.

_____17. Members of the Council of Ancients were required to be married or widowed males over 40 years of age.

_____18. Gracchus Babeuf and his followers protested against equalities in French society.

_____19. Napoleon's armies spread ideas from the French Revolution throughout Europe.

_____20. Napoleon opposed the Coup of Brumaire.

———— 21. Abbe Seiyes was named First Consul.

———— 22. The Constitution of the Year VIII was approved by French voters by a three million to fifteen hundred margin.

———— 23. In 1802 Napoleon was named First Consul for life.

———— 24. Napoleon paid government bureaucrats a high salary so they would be loyal to him.

————25. Napoleon and France were at the height of their power in 1815.

FILL-IN-THE-BLANKS: Write the appropriate word(s) to complete the sentence. The correct answers are given at the end of the chapter.

1. _____ consisted of everybody in France except clergy and aristocrats.

2. _____ were members of the Second Estate whose position was inherited from generation to generation.

3. _____ were members of the Second Estate who had achieved their position by purchase from the monarchy.

4. _____ is a general term that refers to the bankers, lawyers, doctors, storekeepers, and others who provided much of the leadership during the French Revolution.

5. _____ was the French national legislature comprised of representatives from three broad social classes in France.

6. _____ was a vow by representatives of the Third Estate not to adjourn the National Assembly until France had a republican constitution.

7. _____ was the hero of the American Revolution who was given command of the Paris Militia.

8. _____ proclaimed that all French men had the natural rights of liberty, property, security, and resistance to oppression.

9. _____ was Louis XVI's chief financial officer whose dismissal precipitated the attack on the Bastille.

10. _____ was an English woman who wrote *Vindication of the Rights of Women* in 1792.

11. _____ was the name given to French citizens who wanted to restore the monarchy.

12. _____ were males who paid taxes equivalent to three days of wages at the local labor rates under the 1791 Constitution.

13. _____ enacted by the National Assembly, made the Roman Catholic Church a branch of the secular government.

14. _____ were clergymen who refused to swear an oath to support the 1791 Constitution.

15. _____ was the name given to radical Jacobins who originated from the Department of Gironde.

16. _____ were worthless paper notes used by the French revolutionary government to pay its debts.

17. _____ began on September 2 when mobs of Parisians attacked jails and prisons that held individuals thought to be enemies of the revolution.

18. _____ was the British statesman who argued that the French Revolution represented application of a blind form of rationalism that posed a danger to all European society.

19. _____ was the government Robespierre wanted to create in which France would be a democratic nation populated by citizens who exhibited an unselfish public spirit and civic zeal and who personally led a morally upright life.

20. _____ was a battle fought in October 1814 in which Napoleon's army was defeated by the European coalition allied against France.

21. _____ was the island Napoleon was exiled to after his defeat at Waterloo.

22. _____ was a military campaign waged by Napoleon in Spain beginning in 1808 and lasting for five years.

23. _____, issued by England, required all neutral ships carrying trade goods for France or a satellite nation to stop at a British port and pay custom duties.

24. _____ was the English admiral who defeated France at the Battle of Trafalgar.

25. _____ was a series of changes enacted in France from 1804 to 1810 that gave France a uniform legal system.

MULTIPLE CHOICE: Circle the correct response. The correct answers are given at the end of the chapter.

1. What was the spark that ignited the French Revolution?
    a. The passage of laws requiring all French citizens to serve in the military.
    b. Financial bankruptcy of the French monarchy.
    c. French support for American colonists in the American Revolution.
    d. Rioting that occurred in various French cities.

2. Who was the French king beheaded during the French Revolution?
    a. Louis XVI.
    b. George III.
    c. Henry VIII.
    d. Louis XVIII.

3. A French citizen who worked as a banker would likely belong to which of the following:
    a. The First Estate.
    b. The Second Estate.
    c. The Third Estate.
    d. The Fourth Estate.

4. An aristocrat in the Old Regime would be a member of
    a. The First Estate.
    b. The Second Estate.
    c. The Third Estate.
    d. The Fourth Estate.

5. Which one of the following was not a cause of peasant unrest prior to the outbreak of the French Revolution?
    a. Inflation.
    b. Feudal Dues.
    c. Church tithes.
    d. High prices for agricultural produce.

6. What united all laborers prior to the outbreak of the French Revolution?
   a. Fear of unemployment and starvation.
   b. High prices they had to pay for manufactured goods.
   c. The threat that mechanization would take away their jobs.
   d. Fear of a peasant rebellion.

7. Which of the following classes provided leadership for the French Revolution?
   a. Urban factory workers.
   b. Rural peasants.
   c. Bourgeois members of the Third Estate.
   d. Nobles unhappy with the monarchy.

8. Why did aristocrats want to require that each of the three estates have the same number of representatives regardless of its population?
   a. To limit the power of the First Estate which was the most populous of the three estates.
   b. To limit the power of the Second Estate, which was the most influential of the three estates.
   c. To increase the power of the First Estate.
   d. To limit the power of the Third Estate, which was the largest of the three estates.

9. Which one of the following was not contained in the cashiers de doleances?
   a. A complaint about high taxes.
   b. A complaint about unfair fees.
   c. A grievance about aristocratic privileges.
   d. A demand that the Estates General be abolished.

10. Which one of the following was perhaps the most celebrated event in the French Revolution?
    a. Fall of the Bastille.
    b. The Execution of Queen Marie Antoinette.
    c. The Great Fear.
    d. The White Fear.

11. What did the Peasant uprising during the Great Fear ultimately do?
    a. Cause the execution of Louis XVIII.
    b. Destroy remaining vestiges of the feudal regime in France.
    c. Led to the fall of Robespierre.
    d. Gave rise to the dictatorship of Napoleon Bonaparte.

12. What was the most important result of the "Night of August 4"?
    a. Napoleon gained power.
    b. All French citizens became equal under the law.
    c. Louis XVI was executed.
    d. The Estates General was abolished.

13. What did the *Declaration of the Rights of Man and Citizen* do?
    a. Gave French women the right to vote.
    b. Allowed Louis XVI to be executed.
    c. Identified individual and group rights that the French government would respect.
    d. Created the First, Second, and Third Estates.

14. What did *The Rights of Women* do?
    a. Applied the same rights to women that men had.
    b. Prevented women from divorcing men.
    c. Forbade women from working outside the home.
    d. Denied women access to higher education.

15. Under the 1791 Constitution, which of the following classes of citizen could vote.
    a. Passive citizens.
    b. Active citizens.
    c. Emigres.
    d. Women.

16. What did passage of the Civil Constitution of the Clergy do?
    a. Gain church support for the French Revolution.
    b. Give French priests more control over their parish churches.
    c. Eliminated government control over the Roman Catholic Church.
    d. Cause relations between the Catholic Church and the French government to deteriorate.

17. Which of the following best describes the Committee of Public Safety?
    a. It made the French government more democratic.
    b. It was established to create universal male and female suffrage.
    c. It was really a dictatorship.
    d. It was created by passage of the *Declaration of the Rights of Man and Citizen*.

18. What was the primary goal of the Society for Revolutionary Women?
    a. To oppose enemies of the Revolution.
    b. To undo the French Revolution.
    c. To overthrow Robespierre.
    d. To bring France under the control of a dictatorship.

19. Which of the following best describes the Thermidorian Reaction?
    a. It represents the most radical phase of the French Revolution.
    b. It came at the beginning of the French Revolution.
    c. It was the most liberal part of the French Revolution.
    d. It was a moderate to conservative stage of the French Revolution.

20. What did the Constitution of 1795 do?
    a. Rejected both democracy and constitutional monarchy in favor of a republic.
    b. Restored the monarchy.
    c. Made Napoleon dictator.
    d. Gave Robespierre the title of emperor.

21. After the Coup of Brumaire, who was named First Consul?
    a. Louis XVI.
    b. Louis XVIII.
    c. Napoleon Bonaparte.
    d. Abbe Sieyes.

22. Which of the following was the most important legacy from Napoleon's reign?
    a. France ultimately conquered Russia and ruled that country until the 20 century.
    b. The Code Napoleon.
    c. A new constitution that gave French citizens a bill of rights.
    d. Establishment of a French colonial empire in North America.

23. What happened at the Battle of Trafalgar?
    a. The French fleet destroyed the English fleet.
    b. Admiral Horatio Nelson destroyed the French fleet.
    c. Admiral Villeneuve won a decisive victory over the English.
    d. The French victory paved the way for an invasion of England.

24. Why did Napoleon create the Continental System?
    a. To bring order to a chaotic European economy.
    b. To export the French Revolution throughout Europe.
    c. To disrupt England's economy while increasing trade with France.
    d. To force the English to purchase French manufactured goods.

25. What marked the onset of Napoleon's decline?
   a. His invasion of England in 1812.
   b. A disastrous military campaign against Russia in 1812.
   c. The institution of the Continental System in 1809.
   d. The invasion of North Africa in 1816.

MATCHING: Match the response in column B with the item in column A.

Column A

____ 1. Louis XVI   ____ 2. Cashiers de doleances
____ 3. Bastille   ____ 4. First Estate
____ 5. Olympe de Gouges   ____ 6. *Declaration of the Rights of Man And Citizen*
____ 7. Jacobins   ____ 8. Declaration of Pillnitz
____ 9. Reign of Terror   ____ 10. sans-cullottes
____ 11. levee en masse   ____ 12. Maximilien Robespierre
____ 13. Committee of Public Safety ____ 14. Jacques Danton
____ 15. Jeunesse doree   ____ 16. Pain d'egalite
____ 17. Crane Brinton   ____ 18. Coup d'etat of Fructidor
____ 19. Treaty of Campo Formio ____ 20. Napoleon Bonaparte
____ 21. Code Napoleon   ____ 22. Organic Articles
____ 23. The Continental System ____ 24. Treaty of Tilsit
____ 25. Waterloo

Column B

a.   A minor Corsican noble who became Emperor of France.
b.   Working people who supported Robespierre's policies because they suffered from inflation.
c.   The King of France who was executed during the French Revolution.
d.   The town in Belgium where Napoleon was defeated by Field Marshall Gebhard von Blucher.
e.   A radical group who established political clubs across France to work toward establishing universal suffrage and abolition of the monarchy.
f.   Author of the *Declaration of the Rights of Women.*
g.   Military conscription program instituted in France by the Committee of Public Safety.
h.   A long list of grievances presented to King Louix XVI by representatives of the Third Estate.

i.   Author of *Anatomy of a Revolution* who coined the tern Thermidorian Reaction.

j.   A twelve-man committee that governed France during the Reign of Terror.

k.   A prison once used to house enemies of the monarchy whose fall became a celebrated event in the French Revolution.

l.   A period in the French Revolution when numerous people were executed.

m.   A treaty between Alexander I and Napoleon Bonaparte that divided Europe between Russia and France.

n.   An event on September 4, 1797 in which Republican Directors, aided by Napoleon, imposed dictatorship on France.

o.   Consisted of Clergymen.

p.   Plain brown wheat bread French patriots were ordered to eat, called equality bread.

q.   A document that set forth individual and group rights that the French government was bound to respect.

r.   A agreement by the Austrian Emperor, Leopold II and the King of Prussia, Frederick Wilhelm II, to send military force to restore the French monarchy if other European powers agreed to support intervention.

s.   A radical who controlled France and tried to create a "Republic of Virtue."

t.   A member of the Committee of Public Safety along with Robespierre and Carnot.

u.   A treaty between Austria and France signed on October 17, 1797 that incorporated Napoleon's ideas on foreign policy.

v.   Gilded youth who carried long sticks they used to beat people suspected of harboring Jacobin views.

w.   A system established by Napoleon to use French control over the European continent to wage economic warfare against England.

x.   A new legal system imposed on France that, among other things, declared all French people equal under the law regardless of wealth and status.

y.   Laws enacted by Napoleon's government in 1802 which subjected Church activities to normal state police regulations.

ESSAY QUESTIONS: (Answer on separate paper)

1.   What caused the French Revolution?
2.   Discuss the effect radicalism had on the French Revolution.
3.   Identify the different phases of the French Revolution. What events were part of each?
4.   What impact did the French Revolution have on European history?
5.   Discuss Napoleon's rise, fall, and legacy.

ANSWERS TO CHAPTER FIFTEEN

TRUE/FALSE:

1-F; 2-F; 3-F; 4-T; 5-F; 6-F; 7-T; 8-T; 9-F; 10-F; 11-T; 12-T; 13-T; 14-F; 15-F; 16-T; 17-T; 18-F; 19-T; 20-F; 21-F; 22-T; 23-T; 24-T; 25-F

FILL-IN-THE-BLANKS:

1. Second Estate; 2. Nobles of the Sword; 3. Nobles of the Robe; 4. Bourgeois; 5. Estates General; 6. Tennis Court Oath; 7. Marquis de Lafayette; 8. *Declaration of the Rights of Man and Citizen*; 9. Necker; 10. Mary Wollstonecraft; 11. Royalists; 12. Active Citizens; 13. Civil Constitution of the Clergy; 14. Refractory Priests; 15. Girondists; 16. Assignats; 17. September Massacres; 18. Edmund Burke; 19. Republic of Virtue; 20. Battle of the Nations; 21. St. Helena; 22. Peninsular Campaign; 23. Orders of Council; 24. Horatio Nelson; 25. Code Napoleon.

MULTIPLE CHOICE:

1-b; 2-a; 3-c; 4-b; 5-d; 6-a; 7-c; 8-d; 9-d; 10-a; 11-b; 12-b; 13-c; 14-a; 15-b; 16-d; 17-c; 18-a; 19-d; 20-a; 21-c; 22-b; 23-c; 24-c; 25-b

MATCHING:

1-c; 2-h; 3-k; 4-o; 5-f; 6-q; 7-e; 8-r; 9-l; 10-b; 11-g; 12-s; 13-j; 14-t; 15-v; 16-p; 17-i; 18-n; 19-u; 20-a; 21-x; 22-y; 23-w; 24-m; 25-d

CHAPTER SIXTEEN

THE INDUSTRIAL REVOLUTION, 1760-1850

IDENTIFICATION: Briefly describe each term.

Enclosure Movement

Cottage Industry

Zollverein

metallurgy

John Kay

Flying Shuttle

James Hargreaves

Spinning Jenny

Richard Arkwright

water frame

Eli Whitney

cotton gin

Edmund Cartwright

Abraham Darby

Thomas Newcomen

James Watt

Matthew Boulton

Richard Trevithick

George Stephenson

The Rocket

Working conditions for children/women

Michael Sadler

Parliamentary Committee 1832

Edwin Chadwick

Robert Peel

Metropolitan Police Act

Peelers/Bobbies

Limited Liability Act of 1855

new middle class

class consciousness

Combination Acts 1799 and 1800

Luddite Riots

Lancashire Riots

Adam Smith

On the Wealth of Nations

Laissez-faire economics

Thomas Malthus

Essay on Population

David Ricardo

Iron law of wages

Principles of Political Economy and Taxation

Utopian Socialism

Henri de Saint Sion

La Nouveau Christianisme/The New Christianity

Charles Fourier

phalanxes

Robert Owen

Book of the New Moral World

Scientific Socialism

The Communist Manifesto

Das Kapital

Karl Marx

Friedrich Engels

TRUE/FALSE: Indicate whether each statement is true (T) or false (F). The correct answers are given at the end of the chapter.

_____1. The Industrial Revolution originated in Great Britain.

_____2. Eastern Europe experienced the most widespread growth in industry.

_____3. All the countries in Europe had a population boom that directly led to the growth of industry.

_____4. The open field agricultural system eventually gave way to the enclosure movement.

_____5. The putting-out system was most common in the textile industry.

_____6. French farmers were more likely to migrate to the cities than British farmers.

_____7. The Zollverein was under the direction of the British government.

_____8. The earliest automation of textile weaving process was the Spinning Jenny.

_____9. George Stephenson is given credit for the modern railway system.

_____10. In the early Industrial Revolution there were no regulations to limit the number of hours in a workweek.

_____11. Edwin Chadwick believed sewer systems would help stop the spread of disease in cities.

_____12. The Public Health Act of 1848 created a National Board of Health.

_____13. Michael Sadler began a campaign to help improve working conditions.

_____14. Edwin Chadwick helped provide relief for the impoverished as required by the British Poor Law.

_____15. The 1855 Limited Liability Act included only businesses with twenty-five or more employees.

_____ 16. Unskilled laborers lacked the bargaining power for high wages, therefore they were more in demand for factory labor.

_____17. Ned Ludd was the leader of a group that broke many machines.

_____18. The laissez-faire theory is fully compatible with mercantilism.

_____19. Adam Smith believed that competition was harmful to the economy and the wealth of a nation.

_____20. Malthus' proposed that having fewer children would help strengthen the economy.

_____21. Utopian socialists believed that competition was harmful to the economy of a nation.

_____22. Saint Simon was a factory owner who gave up his factory to open a commune.

_____23. Fourier believed in organizing society from the top down, with a strong centralized government.

_____24. Karl Marx is the most well-known Utopian socialist.

_____25. Marxism calls for a necessarily violent uprising by the working class.

FILL-IN-THE-BLANKS: Write the appropriate word(s) to complete the sentence. The correct answers are given at the end of the chapter.

1. The country that led the way in the Industrial Revolution was _____.

2. The cottage industry was also called the _____ system.

3. The _____ was a German trade union.

4. Hargreaves device, _____, was able to spin thread from wool or cotton.

5. In 1785 _____ invented a working power loom, based on earlier models.

6. Darby's method of smelting iron produced a product called _____.

7. _____ improved the Newcomen engine by eliminating the need to cool the cylinder.

8. Compact houses built in cities in long rows were called _____.

9. The Public Health Act of 1848 created the _____.

10. Robert Peel held the office of _____ in Great Britain.

11. During the Industrial Revolution, the two groups that clearly emerged were _____ and _____.

12. The industrial middle class is also called the industrial _____.

13. The word _____ means someone who does not like technology.

14. The _____ sentenced convicted machine breakers to death.

15. According to Adam Smith, if government stays out of the free market economy, national wealth will be _____.

16. Smith, Ricardo, and Malthus are collectively referred to as the _____ of Economics.

17. David Ricardo's thesis is known as the _____.

18. Henri Saint Simon's best known book is _____ ,which argued that helping the poor was basic to Christianity.

19. In Fourier's ideal socialistic society communal living units called _____ would house between 1600 – 1800 people.

20. Robert Owen denounced marriage in his book _____.

21. Owen founded a commune in the town of _____ in Indiana.

22. _____ and _____ wrote *The Communist Manifesto*, published in 1848.

23. Hegel's notion of purposeful change is called the _____.

24. Malthus' book, _____ from 1798 claimed that food supplies are limited and population will continue to expand.

25. According to Marxist theory, there will be a struggle between the _____ and the _____ that will end in a classless society.

MULTIPLE CHOICE: Circle the correct response. The correct answers are given at the end of the chapter.

1. The earliest phase of the Industrial Revolution affected:
   a. Eastern Europe
   b. United States
   c. Western Europe
   d. Southern Europe

2. The enclosure movement:
   a. was known as the open field system
   b. freed serfs in Russia
   c. resulted from the growing population
   d. continued feudalism

3. The putting out system was most common in the _____:
   a. coal industry
   b. textile industry
   c. steel industry
   d. railroad industry

4. All of the following were important to Great Britain's lead except:
   a. cottage industry
   b. chemical industry
   c. standard tax system
   d. credit and banking

5. The first country on the continent to industrialize was:
   a. France
   b. Belgium
   c. Great Britain
   d. Germany

6. All the following caused Germany to lag behind industrially except:
   a. serfdom
   b. separate legal systems
   c. the enclosure movement
   d. internal tariffs

7. The flying shuttle for the hand loom was invented by:
   a. James Hargreaves
   b. Richard Arkwright
   c. James Watt
   d. John Kay

8. Early iron makers used _____ to smelt iron ore:
   a. steam
   b. pig iron
   c. wood
   d. charcoal

9. The inventor of the locomotive called the Rocket was:
   a. Richard Trevithick
   b. George Stephenson
   c. Thomas Newcomen
   d. James Watt

10. The country known as the "workshop of the world" was:
    a. France
    b. Germany
    c. Great Britain
    d. Russia

11. Sadler's Parliamentary Committee wanted to:
    a. improve conditions for child laborers
    b. require owners to pay women higher wages
    c. both of the above
    d. none of the above

12. Chadwick's investigations helped lead to the :
    a. mandatory schooling of English children
    b. Public Health Act
    c. creation of the Peelers
    d. Central Bank of England

13. In the early nineteenth century _____ was the largest of the German states:
    a. Austria
    b. Prussia
    c. Saxony
    d. Belgium

14. Most relocation in the Industrial Revolution was:
    a. urban to rural
    b. due to the new high divorce rate
    c. rural to urban
    d. by serfs in Russia

15. The Peelers:
    a. replaced the constables
    b. immediately spread through the city of London
    c. were established by the Metropolitan Bobbie Act
    d. hit the streets in the late 1850's

16. The Limited Liability Act
    a. allowed businessmen to protect their investments
    b. encouraged investors to take chances on new businesses
    c. helped create managers
    d. all of the above
    e. none of the above

17. The Luddites:
    a. were a legend embodying the frustration of the workers
    b. broke a lot of industrial machinery
    c. destroyed over 1000 power looms at one time
    d. saved the jobs of hundreds of workers

18. According to Adam Smith :
    a. mercantilism is the best economic system
    b. government must remain involved in the economy
    c. even selfish materialism can help propel the economy
    d. each nation should focus only on its own prosperity

19. Malthus made a controversial argument that basically said:
    a. poor people should have fewer children
    b. businessmen should pay the lowest wages possible
    c. supply and demand regulate wages of factory workers
    d. mass produced goods were less efficient than handmade goods

20. The term "Utopian Socialism" was coined by:
    a. Robert Owen
    b. Charles Fourier
    c. Marx and Engels
    d. Henri Saint Simon

21. Which of the following gave up his noble title and became a believer in socialism?
    a. Charles Fourier
    b. Henri Saint Simon
    c. Karl Marx
    d. Robert Owen

22. In Fourier's plan for phalanxes:
    a. the government would subsidize workers' wages
    b. workers changed jobs eight times per day
    c. marriage would be illegal
    d. children only worked ten hours per day

23. Robert Owen's management style included:
    a. hiring children to fold clothes only
    b. reduction of workloads
    c. discouraging education for children
    d. low wages

24. The book _____ launched scientific socialism:
    a. *Book of the New Moral World*
    b. *Das Kapital*
    c. *Dialectical Materialism*
    d. *The Communist Manifesto*

25. The _____ benefitted most from industrialization:
    a. working class
    b. lower class
    c. middle class
    d. upper class

MATCHING: Match the response in column B with the item in column A.

Column A	Column B
_____ 1. Zollverein	a. metro police force
_____ 2. John Kay	b. Marx
_____ 3. Rocket	c. working class
_____ 4. Chadwick	d. Great Britain
_____ 5. Robert Peel	e. middle class
_____ 6. Lancashire	f. flying shuttle
_____ 7. iron law of wages	g. hands off the economy
_____ 8. New Lanark	h. Saint Simon
_____ 9. *Das Kapital*	i. campaign to advance working conditions
_____ 10.workshop of the world	j. Spinning Jenny
_____ 11. Hargreaves	k.German trade union
_____ 12. Michael Sadler	l. outlawed trade unions
_____ 13. Combination Acts	m. sewer system
_____ 14. bourgeoisie	n. Robert Owen
_____ 15. proletariat	o. David Ricardo
_____ 16. *New Christianity*	p. broken power looms
_____ 17. Laissez-faire	q. Stephenson

Match each item in Column A with the most appropriate item in Column B

Column A
_____ 18. Edmund Cartwright
_____ 19. Abraham Darby
_____ 20. Thomas Newcomen
_____ 21. Eli Whitney
_____ 22. Richard Trevithick
_____ 23. Thomas Malthus
_____ 24. Richard Arkwright
_____ 25. Friedrich Engels

Column B (there will be one extra word)
   r. steam engine
   s. pig iron
   t. steam locomotive
   u. water frame
   v. scientific socialist
   w. cotton gin
   x. New Harmony, Indiana
   y. population control
   z. power loom

ESSAY QUESTIONS: (Answer on separate paper)

1. Discuss the reasons why the Industrial Revolution came to Great Britain first. Include in your discussion reasons that impeded growth of industry in other areas such as France and Germany.

2.   Explore the treatment of children during the early Industrial Revolution. Be specific and include details.

3.   Explain why the changing relationship between owners and workers changed during the early Industrial Revolution. What effect do you think this change had on productivity?

4.   Compare and contrast Utopian Socialism with Scientific Socialism.

5.   Discuss Adam Smith's basic idea of how laissez-faire capitalism works and how he believes it benefits a nation.

ANSWERS TO CHAPTER SIXTEEN

TRUE/FALSE:

1-T; 2-F; 3-F; 4-T; 5-T; 6-F; 7-F; 8-F; 9-T; 10-T; 11-T; 12-T; 13-T; 14-T; 15-F; 16-T; 17-F; 18-F; 19-F; 20-T; 21-T; 22-F; 23-F; 24-F; 25-T;

FILL-IN-THE-BLANKS:

1. Great Britain; 2. putting out; 3. Zollverein; 4. Spinning Jenny; 5. Cartwright; 6. pig iron; 7. Watt; 8. row houses; 9. Central or National Board of Health; 10. Home Secretary; 11. laborers and owners; 12. bourgeoisie; 13. Luddite; 14. Frame Breaking Act; 15. maximized; 16. Classical School; 17. iron law of wages; 18. *New Christianity;* 19. phalanxes; 20. *Book of the New Moral World;* 21. New Harmony; 22. Marx and Engels; 23. dialectic; 24. *Essay on Population;* 25. proletariat and bourgeois;

MULTIPLE CHOICE:

1-c; 2-c; 3-b; 4-b; 5-b; 6-c; 7-d; 8-d; 9-b; 10-c; 11-a; 12-b; 13-b; 14-c; 15-a; 16-d; 17-b; 18-c; 19-a; 20-c; 21-b; 22-b; 23-b; 24-d; 25-c;

MATCHING:

1-k; 2-f; 3-q; 4-m; 5-a; 6-p; 7-o; 8-n; 9-b; 10-d; 11-j; 12-i; 13-l; 14-e; 15-c; 16-h; 17-g; 18-z; 19-s; 20-r; 21-w; 22-t; 23-y; 24-u; 25-v;

CHAPTER SEVENTEEN

REACTION, REFORM AND REVOLUTION, 1815-1848

IDENTIFICATION: Briefly describe each term.

Alexander I

Catherine the Great

Congress of Vienna

Klemens von Metternich

Louis XVIII

Principle of Legitimacy

Principle of Restoration

Charles Maurice de Talleyrand

Lord Castlereagh

Concert of Europe

Quadruple Alliance/Quintuple Alliance

Carbonari

Troppau Conference

Ferdinand VII

Carlsbad Decrees

Alexander Ypsilanti

Decembrist Revolt

Northern Society

Southern Society

Six Acts

Corn Laws

"Rotten/Pocket" Boroughs

Reform Bill of 1832

Chartism

Lord Charles Grey

London Working Men's Association

The Northern Star

Charles X

Ultra-royalists

Second French Revolution

Four Ordinances of 1830

Three Glorious Days of July

Louis-Philippe

July Monarchy

William I

Leopold of Saxe-Coburg

Maria Christina

Carlist Wars

1848 Revolutions

Second Republic

Louis Blanc

National Workshops

"Bloody June Days"

June Days Revolution

Louis-Napoleon Bonaparte

Louis Cavaignac

March Laws

Charles Albert

Habsburgs

Magyars

Frederick William IV

Frankfurt Assembly

Romanticism

William Blake

Johann Wolfgang von Goethe

Ludwig van Beethoven

Georg Wilhelm Friedrich Hegel

Dialectic

Karl Marx

The Communist Manifesto

TRUE/FALSE: Indicate whether each statement is true (T) or false (F). The correct answers are given at the end of the chapter.

_____ 1. Historical evidence indicates that Alexander I most definitely faked his death and lived as a hermit monk named Fedor Kuzmich and wandered the Siberian forests for many years.

_____ 2. Karl Marx developed the dialectic.

_____ 3. The Second French Revolution was more radical and more encompassing than the first one.

_____ 4. Liberalism, among other factors, produced the Decembrist Revolt in Russia.

_____ 5. The primary goal of the Congress of Vienna was to restore national and inter national peace.

_____ 6. As a result of the French Revolution and Napoleonic Wars, both the Tory and Whig Parties in England became more liberal.

_____ 7. Universal male suffrage, annual elections for the House of Commons, equal population electoral districts, abolition of property ownership for election to Parliament, and salaries for members of the House of Commons were all demands of the Chartist Movement in England.

_____ 8. During "Bloody June Days" urban guerilla warfare was conducted in Paris.

_____ 9. The election of Louis-Napoleon spelled doom for the Second French Republic.

_____ 10. Prince Klemens von Metternich was forced from power by the 1848 Revolutions in Austria.

_____ 11. Romanticism is such a narrow movement that it is easy to define.

_____ 12. Johann Wolfgang von Goethe was a Romantic musician whose works rivaled Beethoven's in importance.

_____ 13. Francisco Goya is one of the best-known Romantic artists.

_____ 14. Jean Jacques Rousseau's novel _The Sorrows of Young Werther_ is his best-known work.

_____ 15. Karl Marx and Friedrich Engels wrote _The Communist Manifesto_.

_____ 16. Nationalism played little role in the 1848 revolutions in Austria.

_____ 17. The Pan-Slavic Conference in June 1848 rejected political autonomy for Czech nationals.

_____18. In 1839 the Netherlands agreed to recognize Belgium independence.

_____19. In many European nations, the middle class often supported reform and revolution for economic reasons.

_____20. In the years immediately after the Congress of Vienna, conservative, reactionary governments largely crushed liberal movements across Europe.

_____21. Prince Klemens von Metternich dominated the Congress of Vienna.

_____22. Delegates to the Congress of Vienna failed to take steps to ensure that France stayed in its boundaries.

_____23. The most important result of the Congress of Vienna was the territorial boundaries set for various countries by the delegates.

_____24. Over a hundred Decembrists leaders in Russia were exiled to Siberia.

_____25. Thirty-five British demonstrators were killed at the Peterloo Massacre in 1919.

FILL-IN-THE-BLANKS: Write the appropriate word(s) to complete the sentence. The correct answers are given at the end of the chapter.

1. _____ was a movement in art, music, literature, and philosophy that was largely a reaction against the eighteenth century Enlightenment.

2. _____ and _____ were philosophers who opposed the importation of foreign institutions into Germany, maintaining instead that national institutions must be developed from within a country.

3. _____ was a German philosopher who used the dialectic to theorize that the working class would stage a revolution that would create a near perfect society in which private ownership of property was abolished.

4. The _____, written by William Wordsworth and Samuel Taylor Coleridge represent England's greatest contribution to Romantic poetry.

5. The Romantic composer Frederic Chopan wrote many _____ designed to allow peasants to dance to lively tunes.

6. _____ and _____ were the two primary principles that generally guided delegates attending the Congress of Vienna.

7. England, Austria, Prussia, and Russia created the _____ in 1815 to act in concert to quell any rebellion designed to overthrow a legitimately established government.

8. _____ were laws enacted by the German Diet in 1819 that outlawed the Burschenschaften, restricted academic freedom at universities, and imposed press censorship.

9. _____ led a liberal reform movement in Greece that wanted to reestablish the Greek empire that had existed in antiquity.

10. _____ was the leader of Russia who crushed the Decembrists Revolt in 1825.

11. The _____ was legislation passed by the British Parliament designed to prevent demonstrations such as those that led to the Peterloo Massacre.

12. The _____ were enacted by the British Parliament to benefit landlords by levying a high tariff on grain imported into England.

13. _____ was the ultra-royalist French monarch who pursued reactionary policies that touched off the Second French Revolution.

14. _____ was the elected lower house of the French legislature that upset the middle class when interest paid on government bonds was reduced from five to three percent.

15. The _____, issued by Charles X in 1830 dissolved the elected legislature, strictly censored the press, disenfranchised middle class opposition to the royal government, and restricted suffrage in upcoming elections.

16. _____ was the name given to the new French government established as a result of the 1830 Revolution that did not realize the ideas of liberty, equality, and fraternity.

17. _____ was the monarch who ruled the Netherlands in a despotic manner and made Dutch the official language of all the Netherlands even though some of its residents spoke French.

18. _____ had the most liberal government and constitution in all of Europe at the end of the Napoleonic Wars.

19. _____ was the French leader driven into exile by the 1848 Revolution.

20. _____ was a poet who headed a provisional government in France following the abdication of Louis-Philippe.

21. _____ was the name given to a popular welfare project in France whose abolition led to the "Bloody June Days" revolt.

22. The _____, enacted by the Hungarian Parliament in 1848 constitutionally separated Hungary from Austria.

23. _____, the provisional governor of Croatia, defeated Magyar forces, took control of Hungary, and restored Austrian authority in 1848.

24. _____, became Austrian emperor in 1848 after his uncle Ferdinand was deposed. He ruled Austro-Hungary until 1916.

25. _____ became a hero to German rebels in 1848 when he refused to attack rioters in Berlin.

MULTIPLE CHOICE: Circle the correct response. The correct answers are given at the end of the chapter.

1. The meeting held to reconstruct Europe in 1814-15 after the Napoleonic Wars ended was called:
   a. The European Reconstruction Summit.
   b. The European Congress.
   c. The Congress of Vienna.
   d. The Continental Rebuilding League.

2. Who was the Austrian foreign minister who dominated the Congress of Vienna?
   a. Alexander I.
   b. Prince Klemens von Metternich.
   c. Lord Castlereagh.
   d. Charles Maurice de Talleyrand.

3. What two central ideas guided decision making by delegates to the Congress of Vienna?
   a. The principles of legitimacy and restoration.
   b. Greed and territorial gains for their countries.
   c. The desire to punish France and prevent Germany from gaining new territory.
   d. The need to bring Russia into the international community and prevent Austria from gaining new lands.

4. Which of the following statements is most accurate during the years immediately following the Congress of Vienna?
   a. Conservative reactionary governments generally crushed liberal movements across Europe.
   b. Liberal movements generally were successful throughout Europe.
   c. Liberal movements brought much change to Europe in the years immediately after the Congress of Vienna.
   d. Conservative reactionary movements controlled Europe and instituted a "reign of terror" across the continent, executing hundreds of thousands of people.

5. What touched off the Decembrist Revolt of 1825 in Russia?
   a. Activities by French agitators.
   b. The death of Czar Alexander I.
   c. Conservative unhappiness with Czar Alexander I's rule.
   d. The triumph of liberal though in Russia.

6. What political effect did the French Revolution and Napoleonic Wars have on English political parties?
   a. The Whig Party became more liberal.
   b. The Tory Party became more conservative.
   c. Both the Whig and Tory parties became more liberal.
   d. Both the Whig and Tory parties became more conservative.

7. Prior to the 1830s in England, which of the following groups had the most representation in Parliament?
   a. Middle class workers.
   b. Middle class business owners.
   c. Factory workers.
   d. Wealthy landowners.

8. What did the Reform Bill of 1832 do?
   a.   Gave poor workers representation in Parliament.
   b.   Extended the franchise to middle class males and redistributed parliamentary seats.
   c.   Gave control of Parliament to wealthy landowners.
   d.   Extended the franchise to working class men and women and gave labor more representation in Parliament.

9. Which of the following was not a demand of the Chartist Movement?
   a.   Universal suffrage for males and females.
   b.   Annual elections for the House of Commons.
   c.   The secret ballot.
   d.   Equal population electoral districts.

10. Who devised the idea of the dialectic?
   a.   Karl Marx.
   b.   Georg Wilhelm Friedrich Hegel.
   c.   Francisco Goya.
   d.   Fredrich Schlegel.

11. Who is perhaps the best-known Romantic artist?
   a.   John Constable.
   b.   Eugene Delacroix.
   c.   Francisco Goya.
   d.   Leonardo da Vinci

12. Who was perhaps the most important romantic composer?
   a.   Frederic Chopin.
   b.   Ludwig van Beethoven.
   c.   Johannes Sebastian Bach.
   d.   Carl Marie von Weber.

13. What was the most famous work of Johann Wolfgang von Goethe?
   a.   *La Novelle Heloise.*
   b.   *The Sorrows of Young Werther.*
   c.   *The Lyrical Ballads.*
   d.   *Faust.*

14. Which of the following statements is most accurate regarding Romanticism?
    a. It was a reaction against the eighteenth century Enlightenment.
    b. It is a movement that is easy to define.
    c. It rejected all reason and rational thought as a basis of knowledge.
    d. It denied that some knowledge possessed by people was innate.

15. Which of the following was not part of the Four Ordinances of 1830?
    a. The newly elected French legislature was dissolved.
    b. Press censorship.
    c. Middle class opposition to the French government was encouraged.
    d. New elections were ordered held under restricted suffrage.

16. Who did liberal forces in Spain form an alliance with during the 1830 Revolutions?
    a. Queen Maria Christina.
    b. Juan Ponce de Leon.
    c. Don Carlos.
    d. Queen Isabella.

17. At the end of the Napoleonic Wars, which European country had the most liberal government and constitution?
    a. Spain.
    b. England.
    c. France.
    d. Poland.

18. What was the class war that engulfed Paris from June 23 to June 26, 1848 part of?
    a. The June Days Revolution.
    b. The Original French Revolution.
    c. The Liberation of the Bastille.
    d. The Fall of Paris.

19. What played an important part in the Austrian Revolutions of 1848?
    a. A desire to separate from France.
    b. Capitalism.
    c. Nationalism.
    d. Conservative disenchantment with Metternich.

20. Who wrote *La Nouvelle Heloise*?
    a. Napoleon Bonapart.
    b. Jean Jacques Rousseau.
    c. Johann Wolfgang von Goethe.
    d. Lord Byron.

21. Which Polish composer wrote music exclusively for the piano?
    a. Hector Berlioz.
    b. Franz Schubert.
    c. Frederic Chopin.
    d. Johannes Sebastian Bach.

22. Who wrote *The Communist Manifesto*?
    a. Friedrich Hegel.
    b. Karl Marx.
    c. Frederic Chopin.
    d. William Wordsworth.

23. In 1818, Austria, Prussia, Russia, England, and France created the _____ to prevent future revolutions from erupting in Europe.
    a. Quadruple Alliance.
    b. Quintuple Alliance.
    c. Congress of Vienna.
    d. The Anti-Napoleon League.

24. What was the attempt to bring a permanent stability to Europe created as part of the Congress of Vienna called by historians?
    a. The Concert of Europe.
    b. The North Atlantic Treaty Alliance.
    c. The Anti-Revolution League.
    d. The Versailles Peace Agreement.

25. Which one of the following was not a provision of the Carlsbad Decrees?
    a. Censorship of the press.
    b. The Burschenschaften were outlawed.
    c. Academic freedom at universities was restricted.
    d. Individuals were granted freedom of speech.

MATCHING: Match the response in column B with the item in column A.

Column A

_____ 1. Georg Wilhelm Friedrich Hegel
_____ 2. Karl Marx
_____ 3. Eugene Delacroix
_____ 4. Faust
_____ 5. Ludwig van Beethoven
_____ 6. Romanticism
_____ 7. Bloody June Days
_____ 8. Louis-Napoleon
_____ 9. Fedor Kuzmich
_____ 10. Congress of Vienna
_____ 11. Klement von Metternich
_____ 12. Charles Maurice de Talleyrand
_____ 13. Carbonari
_____ 14. Nicholas I
_____ 15. Lord Charles Grey
_____ 16. The Northern Star
_____ 17. Reform Bill of 1832
_____ 18. William Lovett
_____ 19. Prince de Polignac
_____ 20. Carlist Wars
_____ 21. July Revolution
_____ 22. La Nouvelle Heloise
_____ 23. Lyrical Ballads
_____ 24. Hector Berlioz
_____ 25. Fredric Chopin

Column B

a. Wrote the *Requiem*.
b. A novel written by Jean Jacques Rousseau.
c. Dominated Romantic philosophy.
d. Co-author of *The Communist Manifesto*.
e. A Romantic composer who composed exclusively for the piano.
f. Probably the most important Romantic composer.
g. Romantic poetry written by Wordsworth and Coleridge.

h.   Name given to the uprising that occurred in France in 1830.
i.   One of the first artists to exhibit Romantic work.
j.   Russian leader who crushed the Decembrist Revolt.
k.   The most famous work of Johann Wolfgang von Goethe.
l.   A hermit who wandered the forests of Siberia who some believed was really the Russian Czar Alexander I in disguise.
m.   Prime Minister of England from 1830-1834.
n.   A broad movement in art, literature, music, and philosophy that practically defies definition.
o.   Founder of the London Working Men's Association.
p.   A newspaper published by the Chartist Movement to convince English people to support passage of Chartist Reforms.
q.   A class war that engulfed Paris from June 23 to June 26, 1848.
r.   Secret societies of army officers that forced kings in Naples and Spain to accept liberal constitutions.
s.   The Austrian foreign minister who dominated the Congress of Vienna.
t.   Became leader of France and ended the Second French Republic.
u.   Represented France at the Congress of Vienna.
v.   Conflict that occurred in Spain from 1834 to 1840.
w.   A meeting held in Austria during 1814 and 1815 to reconstruct Europe following the Napoleonic Wars.
x.   An Ultra-royalist who claimed to receive mystical visions from the Virgin Mary.
y.   A bill introduced into the English Parliament that extended the franchise to middle class males and provided for the redistribution of parliamentary seats.

ESSAY QUESTIONS: (Answer on separate paper)

1. Write an essay that discusses the importance of the Congress of Vienna in European history during the nineteenth century.
2. Compare and contrast the 1830 revolutions in European countries with the 1848 revolutions. How were they similar? How were they different?
3. Compare and contrast English reaction and reform with reaction and reform on the European continent.
4. Discuss the role Metternich played in suppressing liberalism and revolution throughout Europe.
5. Write an essay that defines Romanticism as it appeared in art, music, literature, and philosophy. Who were the most important figures associated with the Romantic Movement?

ANSWERS TO CHAPTER SEVENTEEN

TRUE/FALSE:

1-F; 2-F; 3-F; 4-T; 5-T; 6-F; 7-T; 8-T; 9-T; 10-T; 11-F; 12-F; 13-T; 14-F; 15-T; 16-F; 17-F; 18-T; 19-T; 20-T; 21-T; 22-F; 23-F; 24-T; 25-F

FILL-IN-THE-BLANKS:

1. Romanticism; 2. Friedrich Schlegel and Friedrich von Savigny; 3. Karl Marx; 4. Lyrical Ballads; 5. polonaises; 6. legitimacy and restoration; 7. Quadruple Alliance 8. Carlsbad Decrees; 9. Alexander Ypsilanti; 10. Nicholas I; 11. Six Acts; 12. Corn Laws; 13. Charles X; 14. Chamber of Deputies; 15. The Four Ordinances; 16. July Monarchy; 17. William I; 18. Poland; 19. Louis-Philippe; 20. Alphonse de Lamartine; 21. National Workshops; 22. March Laws; 23. Count Jellachich; 24. Francis Joseph; 25. King Frederick William IV

MULTIPLE CHOICE:

1-c; 2-b; 3-a; 4-a; 5-b; 6-d; 7-d; 8-b; 9-a; 10-b; 11-c; 12-b; 13-d; 14-a; 15-c; 16-a; 17-d; 18-a; 19-c; 20-b; 21-c; 22-b; 23-b; 24-a; 25-d

MATCHING:

1-c; 2-d; 3-i; 4-k; 5-f; 6-n; 7-q; 8-t; 9-l; 10-w; 11-s; 12-u; 13-r; 14-j; 15-m; 16-p; 17-y; 18-o; 19-x; 20-v; 21-h; 22-b; 23-g; 24-a; 25-e

CHAPTER EIGHTEEN

NATIONALISM & REALPOLITIK 1848-1871

IDENTIFICATION: Briefly describe each term.

<u>Megalomaniac</u>

<u>Hegemony</u>

<u>Constitutional Monarchy</u>

<u>Carbonari</u>

<u>Count Camilo Cavour</u>

<u>Napoleon III</u>

<u>Magyars</u>

<u>Zollverein</u>

<u>Pope Pius IX</u>

Giuseppe Garibaldi

Otto von Bismarck

Paris Commune

Franz Joseph

Crimean War

Reischstag

Junker

Serfs

Archduke Maximillian

Franco Prussian War

Red Shirts

Land and Freedom

Adolphe Theirs

Nationalism

Giuseppi Mazzini

TRUE/FALSE: Indicate whether each statement is true (T) or false (F). The correct answers are given at the end of the chapter.

_____1. Count Cavour did not favor Italian unification.

_____2. Giuseppe Garibaldi was the leader of a group called the Black Shirts.

_____3. Rome became the Italian capital after the Franco Prussian War.

_____4. The Zollverein was a radical German political party.

_____5. Austrian power helped limit German liberal ideas for unification.

_____6. Reorganization of the Prussian army was key to German unification.

_____7. Bismarck determined that domestic reforms would help unite the German states.

_____8. The Prussian victory in the Seven Years War led to its expansion into new territories.

_____9. In the attempt to unite Germany, conservatives were more effective than liberals.

_____10. After Bismarck became prime minister, he was more a conservative than a reactionary.

_____11. The winner of the Franco Prussian war was Napoleon III and France.

_____12. The Danish War of 1864 saw an alliance between Prussia and Austria.

_____13. Bismarck defeated Italy in the war he devised in 1866.

_____14. The Ems Telegraph was a political ploy of Bismarck.

_____ 15. Historians see Napoleon's III reign in two stages.

_____ 16. The Paris Commune was a reaction to the British invasion of French areas.

_____ 17. The Austro-Hungarian empire was inhabited by a basically Germanic group who ruled their minorities benevolently.

_____ 18. Czechs were encouraged by the Germans to develop a national consciousness.

_____ 19. Magyar administration angered other minorities by forcing their culture on them.

_____ 20. In the Crimean War, Czar Nicholas wanted to expand Russian supremacy in the Mediterranean Sea.

_____ 21. When freed, serfs in Russia were each granted a parcel of land.

_____ 22. Alexander tried to institute reforms which would modernize Russia.

_____ 23. One of the results of Alexander's efforts to change Russia was his assassination.

_____ 24. The Third Republic wanted a Bourbon descendant to take the throne of France.

_____ 25. A failed policy that would add to the downfall of Napoleon III was his policies in Mexico.

FILL-IN-THE-BLANKS: Write the appropriate word(s) to complete the sentence. The correct answers are given at the end of the chapter.

1. The leading state for Italian unification was _____.

2. The first King of Italy was _____.

3. The leading revolutionary who wanted a republican form of government for Italy was _____.

4. In 1858, _____ of Prussia was declared insane.

5. The _____ was the upper house of the German Legislature.

6. Bismarck believed the biggest enemy for Prussia was _____.

7. By the 1870's Prussia had united all the German states except _____.

8. The famous document that Bismarck corrupted, causing war, was _____

9. In December 1848, _____ was elected president of the Second Republic of France.

10. The radicals of Paris formed the _____.

11. Crisis in the Second Republic caused the formation of the_____, the longest lasting government in France.

12. The Austro-Hungarian empire, controlled by Germans, included many _____.

13. The Prussians defeated the French in 1866 at _____.

14. In Hungary, minority groups had _____ rights of citizenship,.

15. The Russian government, compared to Western governments, was _____.

16. Czarist Russia's official doctrine was that the Czar ruled _____.

17. The Crimean War demonstrated nationalism translated into _____.

18. In the Crimean War, England fought to protect _____ as well as their own interests.

19. France was allied with _____ during the Crimean war.

20. In 1861, Alexander II of Russia _____.

21. After the Crimean War, European affairs were _____.

22. Alexander II of Russia tried to "russify" _____.

23. A radical newspaper about Russian politics, published in England, was _____.

24. The _____ was Alexander's secret police.

25. Great Britain, during this period, symbolized _____.

MULTIPLE CHOICE: Circle the correct response. The correct answers are given at the end of the chapter.

1. One of the Italian revolutionary groups was called
    a. the Pintos
    b. the Ramones
    c. the Carbonari
    d. the Brothers

2. Count Cavour formed alliances with
    a. Spain and Italy
    b. England and France
    c. Austria
    d. did not make alliances

3. Cavour's office was
    a. king of Tuscany
    b. chief minister of the Piedmont.
    c. Prime Minister of Italy
    d. Prince of Sicily

4. Giuseppe Garibaldi began his fight for Italian unification in
    a. Rome
    b. Spain
    c. Venice
    d. Sicily

5. In 1861, the king of Italy was
    a. Napoleon III
    b. Count Cavour
    c. Victor Emmanuel
    d. Czar Nicholas.

6. Italy gained the territory of Venezia after the
   a. Anglo American war
   b. Franco Prussian war;
   c. negotiations with the Venetians
   d. Peach of Westerfield.

7. The German states organized a customs union called the
   a. Zollverein
   b. the Association
   c. the Gestapo
   d. the Patriotic German union

8. The leading state in the unification of Germany was
   a. Bavaria
   b. Austria
   c. Prussia
   d. Moldavia

9. Bismarck believed a strong Prussia needed
   a. a democratic government
   b. a divine right king
   c. Parliamentary control of the army
   d. all of the above

10. The Prussian victory at Sadow
    a. defeated Austria
    b. defeated France
    c. was meaningless
    d. saw the death of Bismarck

11. The hold out German states were in the
    a. North
    b. South
    c. East
    d. West

12. Bismarck had hopes for war between Prussia and
    a. France
    b. Great Britain
    c. Austria
    d. Russia

13. Bismarck edited the Ems telegram
    a. because it made no sense
    b. he didn't like the way it was written
    c. it was not in German
    d. to anger the Prussian government

14. As a result of the Franco Prussian War
    a. Bismarck was defeated
    b. Napoleon III was imprisoned
    c. money was paid to England
    d. Prussia lost her influence over Germany

15. Napoleon's III policies changed from
    a. liberal to conservative
    b. conservative to liberal
    c. supporting Alexander II's claim to India
    d. wanting to be king but settling to be president

16. The Treaty of Frankfurt allowed
    a. Napoleon III to be emperor
    b. Bismarck to be king of Germany
    c. Great Britain to rule Prussia
    d. Prussian troops to occupy France.

17. The confusion over who would become king of Spain in 1870 led to
    a. the rise of the Spanish guard
    b. a native uprising in Grenoble
    c. the Franco Prussian War
    d. Napoleon's heir claiming the English throne.

18. In the Hapsburg Empire, Franz Joseph
    a. was an inept ruler
    b. went insane
    c. married Bismarck's daughter
    d. ruled for over 50 years.

19. The majority ethnic culture in Hungary was
    a. the Magyars
    b. the Huns
    c. the Austrians
    d. the Germans.

20. For many years in Russia, progressive movements of Western Europe
    a. were easily adapted to new ideas
    b. remained untouched by Western ideas
    c. sent many scholars abroad
    d. were basically changed to Western ideals.

21. The Russian czar Nicholas I emphasized
    a. the rights of serfs
    b. the power of his prime minister
    c. the divine right theory
    d. cooperation with Western liberals.

22. In the Crimean War, Russia fought against
    a. China
    b. Crimea
    c. England
    d. Spain.

23. Alexander's purpose in emancipating the Russian serfs was to
    a. live up to noble ideals his mother taught him
    b. utilize Russian resources better
    c. get them to leave the country and go to China
    d. make them political allies against his traditional nobles.

24. The major reforms that Alexander brought to Russia referred to
    a. Marxist ideas
    b. the judicial system
    c. the polygamy of the nobility
    d. the idea that the czar was just a citizen.

25. The "Land and Freedom" movement took place in
    a. England
    b. Russia
    c. France
    d. Italy.

MATCHING: Match the response in column B with the item in column A.

_____ 1. Zollverein
_____ 2. Alexander II
_____ 3. Junkers
_____ 4. Divine Right Theory
_____ 5. Crimean War
_____ 6. Otto von Bismarck
_____ 7. Francis Joseph
_____ 8. Ottoman Empire
_____ 9. Giuseppe Garibaldi
_____ 10. Red Shirts

_____ 11. Paris Commune
_____ 12. Hall of Mirrors
_____ 13. Land and Freedom
_____ 14. Serfs
_____ 15. Reischstag
_____ 16. Archduke Maximillian
_____ 17. Third Republic of France
_____ 18. Bad Ems
_____ 19. Marxists
_____ 20. Franco Prussian War
_____ 21. Victor Emmanuel

A. Turkish rule in the Middle East and Balkans
B. Magyars
C. Russia wars with Britain and France
D. Prussian Leader
E. End of second French Republic
F. kings appointed by God
G. Austrian rulers
H. French government in Mexico
I. Italian fighters for national unity
J. City where the meeting about accession to the Spanish throne took place
K. German States association
L. First king of Italy
M. Early Communists
N. French radicals
O. Farmers with no political rights or land
P. Prussian noble
Q. Italian freedom fighter
R. Russian radical group
S. Habsburg dynasty
T. German Empire proclaimed
U. Fall of Napoleon III

_____ 22. Carbonari
_____ 23. Habsburg
_____ 24. Czar
_____ 25. Hungarian majority

V. Russian leader
W. Italian revolutionaries
X. Lower house of the German legislature
Y. freed Russian serfs

ESSAY QUESTIONS: (Answer on separate paper)

1. German and Italian unification had many things in common. Both their early leaders were conservatives. How could "conservatives" change the map of Europe so drastically?

2. What is "nationalism" and how did it change the "face" of Europe?

3. How did Louis Napoleon get elected to the presidency of the Second French Republic?

4. What policies did Alexander II pursue? What were the results?

5. Compare and contrast the ideologies of conservatism and liberalism.

ANSWERS TO CHAPTER EIGHTEEN

TRUE/FALSE:

1-F; 2-F; 3-F; 4-F; 5-T; 6-T; 7-F; 8-T; 9-T; 10-T; 11-F; 12-T; 13-F; 14-T; 15-T; 16-F; 17-F; 18-F; 19-T; 20-T; 21-F; 22-T; 23-T; 24-F; 25-T

FILL-IN-THE-BLANKS:

1. Piedmont; 2. Victor Emmanuel 3. G. Mazzini 4. Frederick William IV 5. Bundesreich
6. Austria 7. Southern states. 8. the Ems Telegraph 9. Louis Napoleon 10. Paris Commune
11. The Third Republic 12 mino.rities 13. Battle of Kniggratz14. limited
15. backward 16. by divine right 17., imperialism 18. Turkey 19. England 20. freed the serfs
21. unstable 22. Poland 23. The Bell 24. Okhrana 25. a confident liberal state.

MULTIPLE CHOICE:

1-c; 2-b; 3-b; 4-d; 5-c; 6-b; 7-a; 8-c; 9-b; 10-c; 11-b; 12-a; 13-d; 14-b; 15-b; 16-d; 17-c; 18-d; 19-a; 20-b; 21-c; 22-c; 23-c; 24-b; 25-b

MATCHING:

1-K; 2-Y; 3-P; 4-F; 5-C; 6-D; 7-S; 8-A; 9-Q; 10-W; 11-N; 12-T; 13-R; 14-O; 15-X; 16-H; 17-E; 18-J; 19-M; 20-U; 21-L; 22-I; 23-G; 24-V; 25-B

CHAPTER NINETEEN

LA BELLE EPOCH: EUROPE'S GOLDEN AGE 1971-1914

IDENTIFICATION: Briefly describe each term.

Alfred Dreyfus

Emile Zola

The Second Industrial Revolution

The Descent of Man

On the Origin of Species

Humanistic Religion

Friedrich Nietzsche

nineteenth century liberalism

Benjamin Disraeli

Leo Tolstoy

Karl Marx

Friedrich Engels

V. I. Lenin

Bolsheviks

Mensheviks

anarchism

Married Women's Property Act of 1893

Impressionism

Claude Monet

Bourgeoisie

Proletariat

National Union of Women's Suffrage Societies

Claude Debussy

Women's Social and Political Union

Revised Marxism/socialism

conspicuous consumption

the Balkans

Auguste Comte

Sigmund Freud

Congress of Berlin (1878)

Pan-Slavs

Charles Darwin

Social Darwinism

Alexander II

October Manifesto

League of Three Emperors

the Third Republic

status quo ante bellum

Russian Baltic fleet

Dogger Bank Incident

Father Gapon

suffragettes

Emmeline Pankhurst

Wilhelm I

Otto von Bismarck

Kulturkampf

Wilhelm II

Franz Joseph

Nicholas II

"the White Man's Burden"

Scramble for Africa

The Battle of Tsushima

Reichstag

Bloody Sunday

Education Act of 1870

The Duma

Boer Wars

The Irish Question

Boxer Protocol of 1901

TRUE/FALSE: Indicate whether each statement is true (T) or false (F). The correct answers are given at the end of the chapter.

_____1. Europe's Golden Age began in 1914.

_____2. Bolshevik means majority in Russian.

_____3. Renoir was a modernist musician.

105

_____4. Great Britain made great progress toward democracy during the Golden Age.

_____5. Imperialism can mean simply control of one people by another.

_____6. *The White Man's Burden* is a novel about European imperialism.

_____7. Nietzsche represents romanticism in literature.

_____8. Emile Zola is an example of a Naturalist author.

_____9. Cezanne was an Impressionist.

_____ 10. *Conspicuous consumption* implies that you should save for an emergency.

_____ 11. "Higher criticism" of the Bible means to apply scientific methods to determine its accuracy.

_____ 12. Charles Darwin coined the phrase "Social Darwinism."

_____ 13. The id is a person's conscience and is responsible for curbing our most primal urges.

_____ 14. *Return of the Native* represents Realism in literature.

_____ 15. By the early twentieth century, women in Germany could not work outside the home without permission of the husband.

_____ 16. Millicent Fawcett's group believed in using any means possible to achieve suffrage.

_____ 17. Karl Marx created the iron law of wages.

_____18. Lenin chose the name *Zemvesto* for his group because it meant majority.

_____19. *The People's Will* assassinated the Russian leader in 1881.

_____ 20. In Germany, the members of the *Reichstag* were elected.

_____ 21. Peter Kropotkin supported the Marxist movement in Europe.

_____ 22. The *Kulturkampf* effectively ended the power of the Centre Party in Germany.

_____ 23. Kaiser William I became the first ruler to battle socialism with socialistic programs in Germany.

_____ 24. The zemvesto law turned France into 360 local districts.

_____ 25. The Boxer Protocol of 1901 allowed Europeans to leave troops in Japan and to build military bases in Japanese territory.

FILL-IN-THE-BLANKS: Write the appropriate word(s) to complete the sentence. The correct answers are given at the end of the chapter.

1. The German word for culture war is _____.

2. The Chancellor who instituted the culture war against the Catholic Church was _____.

3. Darwin's famous book from 1869,_____, spelled out a theory of "survival of the fittest" in nature.

4. Subjecting the Bible to scientific methods is called _____.

5. The philosopher, _____ ,applied Darwin's ideas to societies and individuals in Social Darwinism.

6. _____ is known as the founder of sociology.

7. The _____part of personality constantly seeks pleasure according to Sigmund Freud.

8. Gustave Flaubert wrote the realist novel _____.

9. What country was known as the workshop of the world? _____

10. In Great Britain, the _____ gave a certain group of women the right to own private property.

11. The _____was founded by Emmeline Pankhurst and her daughters to advance women's rights.

12. _____ was an early leader of the Bolshevik faction, who eventually changed the group's name to Communist Party.

13. William II refused to renew the _____ with Russia in 1890, even though Bismarck supported the renewal.

14. One of William Gladstone's early reforms was the _____, which, among other things, formed local school boards.

15. The author of *The Future of an Illusion* was _____.

16. The British and the Dutch signed the _____ at the end of the Boer Wars.

17. Rumors of abuse of Christians by Muslims in the Ottoman Empire can be lumped together and referred to as _____.

18. The name of the Russian Parliament created by Nicholas in 1905 is _____.

19. Abyssinia is called _____ today.

20. The native Hungarians who tried to keep some control of their government after the *Ausgleich* were the _____.

21. The Japanese attacked the Russian base at _____ starting the Russo Japanese War.

22. Otto von Bismarck was also known as the _____.

23. Kaiser _____ asked for Bismarck's resignation.

24. The Impressionist painter who is known for his studies of water lilies is _____.

25. Russia, Austria-Hungary, and Germany had an alliance called _____.

MULTIPLE CHOICE: Circle the correct response. The correct answers are given at the end of the chapter.

1. Who wrote *Thus Spoke Zarathustra*?
    a. Auguste Comte
    b. Friedrich Nietzsche
    c. Sigmund Freud
    d. Friedrich Engels

2. The "Iron Chancellor" of Germany spent most of his career politically
   a. socialist
   b. liberal
   c. conservative
   d. anarchist

3. Which of the following governmental systems did Nicholas II favor?
   a. communist
   b. democratic
   c. monarchial
   d. anarchist

4. _____ passed the Reform Act to extend male suffrage.
   a. Germany
   b. Britain
   c. France
   d. Austria-Hungary

5. Alfred Dreyfus was a member of the military in what country?
   a. Germany
   b. Britain
   c. France
   d. Russia

6. The Third Republic was the government of
   a. Germany
   b. Britain
   c. France
   d. Russia

7. Who was not an Impressionist painter?
   a. Renoir
   b. Monet
   c. Manet
   d. Cezanne

8. "Home Rule" was a problem for which country?
   a. France
   b. Great Britain
   c. Germany
   d. Russia

9. Which country chose not to colonize Africa during the "Scramble for Africa"?
   a. Germany
   b. Russia
   c. Britain
   d. Italy

10. Russia's minister of finance who helped build up Russian industry was
    a. Fydor Dostoyevsky
    b. Sergei Witte
    c. Nicholas II
    d. Father Gapon

11. A group that sought unity among Slavic peoples was
    a. Ottoman Slavs
    b. Pan Slavs
    c. Bulgarian Slavs
    d. Boxer Slavs

12. Which of the following men was a socialist?
    a. William Gladstone
    b. Friedrich Engels
    c. William I
    d. William II

13. Alfred Dreyfus was sentenced to prison at
    a. Alcatraz
    b. San Quentin
    c. Devil's Island
    d. Suez Canal

14. The incident where Russian ships fired on peaceful British fishing boats is known as
    a. the Anglo-Russian War
    b. the Dogger Bank Incident
    c. the Battle of Tsushima
    d. Bloody Sunday

15. Who led the protest to the Czar's Winter Palace in 1905?
    a. Father Gapon
    b. Sergei Witte
    c. Peter Stolypin
    d. V.I. Lenin

16. The monarch over the Dual Monarchy of Austria-Hungary was
    a. Franz Ferdinand
    b. Franz Joseph
    c. Alexander III
    d. Emile Zola

17. Who believed sociology was the "ultimate science"?
    a. Sigmund Freud
    b. Friedrich Nietzsche
    c. Auguste Comte
    d. Herbert Spencer

18. After the Franco-Prussian War, Germany took what territory from France?
    a. Alsace-Lorraine
    b. Sedan
    c. Suez Canal
    d. English Channel

19. Which of these is NOT a characteristic of 19th century liberalism?
    a. free trade
    b. individualism
    c. repressive trade policies
    d. expanded suffrage

20. The National Union of Women's Suffrage Societies was led by
    a. Emmeline Pankhurst
    b. Eleanor Roosevelt
    c. Queen Victoria
    d. Millicent Fawcett

21. The Factory and Workshops Act did which of the following?
    a. allowed peaceful picketing
    b. allowed a maximum 10-hour workday
    c. allowed for labor unions
    d. allowed lawsuits against employers

22. The British "home rule" problem involved which of the following?
    a. Boers
    b. Scots
    c. Irish
    d. Transvaals

23. The reform acts did what?
    a. created health insurance
    b. expanded suffrage
    c. required school attendance until age 14
    d. removed British influence in South Africa

24. What was the sick man of Europe?
    a. the Ottoman Empire
    b. the British Empire
    c. the Russian Empire
    d. the Austro-Hungarian Empire

25. Who forced Bismarck's resignation?
    a. Disraeli
    b. William I
    c. Gladstone
    d. William II

MATCHING: Match the person with the appropriate country. *Most* countries will be used more than once.

_____ 1. Alexander III   a. Great Britain
_____ 2. Michael Bakunin   b. France
_____ 3. Peter Kropotkin   c. Germany
_____ 4. Alfred Dreyfus   d. Russia
_____ 5. Benjamin Disraeli   e. Austria Hungary
_____ 6. Otto von Bismarck
_____ 7. William II
_____ 8. Friedrich Nietzsche
_____ 9. William Gladstone
_____ 10. Nicolas II
_____ 11. Emmeline Pankhurst
_____ 12. Father Gapon
_____ 13. Peter Stolypin
_____ 14. Sergei Witte
_____ 15. Franz Joseph
_____ 16. Herbert Spencer
_____ 17. Thomas Hardy

Match each item in Column A with the most appropriate item in Column B

Column A   **Column B (there will be one extra word)**

_____ 18. Social Darwinism   a. zemvesto
_____ 19. Impressionism   b. Michael Bakunin
_____ 20. Anarchy   c. Renoir
_____ 21. The Communist Manifesto   d. Friedrich Engels
_____ 22. Port Arthur   e. Herbert Spencer
_____ 23. Gregory Clause   f. Factory and Workshops Act
_____ 24. Benjamin Disraeli   g. Irish Question
_____ 25. Boers   h. South Africa
                                  i. Russo Japanese War

ESSAY QUESTIONS: (Answer on separate paper)

1. Discuss the effect Charles Darwin's theories of evolution and natural selection had on the fields of sociology and psychology.
2. Discuss the major accomplishments of Liberalism in the nineteenth century.
3. Explain how and why original Marxism had to be revised in the late nineteenth century.

ANSWERS TO CHAPTER NINETEEN

TRUE/FALSE:

1-F; 2-T; 3-F; 4-T; 5-T; 6-F; 7-F; 8-T; 9-F; 10-F; 11-T; 12-F; 13-F; 14-T; 15-F; 16-F; 17-F; 18-F; 19-T; 20-T; 21-F; 22-F; 23-F; 24-F; 25-F

FILL-IN-THE-BLANKS:

1.   Kulturkampf 2. Otto von Bismarck 3. On the Origin of Species 4. higher criticism
5.   Herbert Spencer 6. Auguste Comte 7. Id 8. Madame Bovary 9. Great Britain
10. Married Women's Property Act 11. Women's Social and Political Union 12. Lenin
13. Reinsurance Treaty 14. Education Act of 1870 15. Sigmund Freud 16. Treaty of Vereeniging
17. Bulgarian Horrors 18. Duma 19. Ethiopia 20. Magyars 21. Port Arthur
22. Iron Chancellor 23. William II 24. Claude Monet 25. Three Emperor's League

MULTIPLE CHOICE:

1-b; 2-c; 3-c; 4-b; 5-c; 6-c; 7-d; 8-b; 9-b; 10-b; 11-b; 12-b; 13-c; 14-b; 15-a; 16-b; 17-c; 18-a; 19-c; 20-d; 21-b; 22-c; 23-b; 24-a; 25-d

MATCHING:

1-d; 2-d; 3-d; 4-b; 5-a; 6-c; 7-c; 8-c; 9-a; 10-d; 11-a; 12-d; 13-d; 14-d; 15-e; 16-a; 17-a; 18-e; 19-c; 20-b; 21-d; 22-i; 23-g; 24-f; 25-h

CHAPTER TWENTY

THE GREAT WAR 1914-1919

IDENTIFICATION: Briefly describe each term.

Francis Ferdinand

Gavrilo Princip

Otto von Bismarck

Realpolitik

Kaiser Wilhelm II

Nicholas II

First Balkan War

Young Turks

Second Balkan War

Dreadnought

Black Hand

Blank Check

Schlieffen Plan

Joseph Joffre

First Battle of the Marne

Christmas Truce

Paul von Hindenberg

Erich Ludendorff

Battle of Tanenberg

Gallipoli

Mustafa Kemal

Verdun

Erich von Falkenhayn

Henri Petain

Battle of the Somme

Pal Regiments

Georges Clemenceau

David Lloyd George

Lawrence of Arabia

Shell Shock

Trench Warfare

Passchendaele

Total War

Big Berthas

Britain Prepared

Heart of the World

Pankhursts

WAAC's

Easter Rebellion

Rasputin

Leon Trotsky

March Revolution

Order No. 1

Alexander Kerensky

Vladimir Lenin

Bolshevik Revolution

April Theses

Constituent Assembly

Treaty of Brest-Litovsk

Woodrow Wilson

U-boat

Lusitania

Unrestricted submarine warfare

John Pershing

Second Battle of the Marne

Fourteen Points

League of Nations

Big Four

Treaty of Versailles

War reparations

War Guilt Clause

TRUE/FALSE: Indicate whether each statement is true (T) or false (F). The correct answers are given at the end of the chapter.

_____1. Otto von Bismarck assassinated Francis Ferdinand.

_____2. Kaiser Wilhelm II's decision to drop the Reinsurance Treaty with Russia was a mistake.

_____3. England and Russia settled all their colonial disputes by signing the Entente Cordiale.

_____4. Germany's "blank check" assured France that it could take any action deemed appropriate to punish Austria.

_____5. When World War I broke out, patriotism overcame class and other internal conflicts in most European countries.

_____6. Great Britain, France, and Russia were members of the Triple Entente.

_____7. Germany, Austria-Hungary, and the Ottoman Empire were members of the Triple Alliance.

_____8. A cavalry charge was the only tactic effective enough to drive soldiers out of trenches in World War I.

_____9. Russian forces were defeated at the Battle of Tanenberg.

_____10. Over half of Serbia's population was killed during World War I.

_____11. About 700,000 men were killed or wounded in the ten-month battle at Verdun.

_____12. Pal Regiments consisted of recruits to the British army from the same county or town who were kept together during World War I.

_____13. Lawrence of Arabia was a British officer in Western Europe who devised a plan to win the Battle of the Somme.

_____14. Soldiers during World War I did not experience post-traumatic stress disorder in large numbers.

_____15. Soldiers living in the trenches were generally comfortable and experienced few hardships.

_____16. World War I was the first "total war."

_____17. Individuals in most European countries were free to criticize the war without facing charges of sedition.

_____18. The Pankhursts supported the war in England.

_____19. Thousands of women worked to support the war effort in England and France.

_____20. Rasputin, was the brother of Czar Nicholas II.

_____21. The 350-year-old Russian monarchy collapsed in one week.

_____22. Alexander Kerensky led the Bolshevik Revolution in Russia.

_____23. Lenin, in the "April Theses," maintained that Russia must withdraw from WW I.

_____24. Woodrow Wilson developed the Fourteen Points as a basis for peace negotiations to end World War I.

_____25. The United States did not ratify the Treaty of Versailles.

FILL-IN-THE-BLANKS: Write the appropriate word(s) to complete the sentence. The correct answers are given at the end of the chapter.

1. _____ was the alliance system that included Germany, Austria-Hungary, and Italy.

2. _____ was the alliance system that included Great Britain, France, and Russia.

3. _____ remarked that "the lamps are going out all over Europe: we shall not see them lit again in our lifetime."

4. _____ was known as the Iron Chancellor. He understood that European peace depended on maintaining a balance of power among various nations.

5._____ was an agreement in 1904 in which England and France settled their colonial disputes.

6._____ was known as the "sick man of Europe."

7._____ invented dynamite and a smokeless gunpowder that could propel shells and bullets.

8._____ was the terrorist organization responsible for the assassination of Archduke Francis Ferdinand.

9._____ was the German Chancellor who stated: "Just for the sake of a scrap of paper Great Britain is going to make war on a kindred nation."

10._____ was the Italian Prime Minister who was one of the Big Four at the Versailles Peace Conference.

11._____ was the French Premier who stated, "God gave us the Ten Commandments and we broke them. Wilson gave us his Fourteen Points—we shall see."

12._____ headed the Provisional Russian government after the March Revolution.

13._____ was the spiritual healer who exerted influence over Czarina Alexandra due to his ability to supposedly control the bleeding of her hemophiliac son.

14._____ was the British luxury liner that was sank off the Irish coast by a German U-boat in May 1915.

15._____, fought in September 1914, saw casualties of 40 percent.

16._____ was the Belgian town where German soldiers slaughtered 600 men, women, and children in the village square.

17._____ was a British battleship whose launching in 1906 led to an intensified naval arms race between England and Germany.

18._____ was the Serbian nationalist who assassinated Francis Ferdinand and his wife Sophia.

19._____ is the term used to describe politics that are grounded in realities rather than in ideology.

20._____ was a system of alliances between nations used to maintain European peace from 1815 to 1914.

21._____ was the commander of British and French troops at the First Battle of the Marne.

22._____ was the first lord of the British admiralty who suggested that the Allies break the stalemate in western Europe by attacking the Dardanelles and capturing Constantinople.

23._____ was the American president who attended the Versailles Peace Conference.

24._____ was the international organization created in the Treaty of Versailles to maintain world peace.

25._____ was the name of Woodrow Wilson's plan accepted as the basis of negotiations at the Versailles Peace Conference.

MULTIPLE CHOICE: Circle the correct response. The correct answers are given at the end of the chapter.

1. Otto von Bismarck was a proponent of
   a. Realpolitiks.
   b. Politics grounded in ideology.
   c. Absolute democracy
   d. Republican Government.

2. Kaiser Wilhelm II's decision to drop the Reinsurance Treaty with Russia caused Russia to do what?
   a. Invade Germany.
   b. Attack Poland.
   c. Form a defensive military alliance with France.
   d. Form a defensive military alliance with England and Austria.

3. What was the central country in the European balance of power system?
   a. France.
   b. Russia.
   c. Germany.
   d. England.

4. What did England and France do in the Entente Cordiale?
   a. Declare war on Germany.
   b. Settle all their colonial disputes.
   c. Make a military alliance against Germany and Austria.
   d. Give Germany territory in Central Europe.

5. What was the most volatile part of Europe during the first two decades of the 20th century?
   a. Western Europe.
   b. Russia.
   c. The Balkans.
   d. The Iberian Peninsula.

6. What did Alfred Nobel do?
   a. Invented dynamite and smokeless gunpowder
   b. Won the first Nobel Peace Prize.
   c. Manufactured the first tank.
   d. Mounted the first machine gun on the first airplane.

7. Which of the following statements is most accurate about the public reaction to the outbreak of World War I?
   a. Mass protest marches were held in Germany.
   b. French citizens refused to support their government in the war.
   c. Vast crowds in every European capital celebrated the declaration of war.
   d. Workers did not allow patriotism to interfere with class and other internal conflicts.

8. What was the Christmas Truce?
   a. A temporary truce called by European governments in WW I over the Christmas holidays every year.
   b. A meeting of soldiers between the lines to exchange buttons, badges, and cigarettes on Christmas morning in 1914.
   c. An attempt by Germany to end the war by signing a peace treaty with France and England.
   d. The event that allowed Italy to change sides during World War I.

9. What did success of the Schlieffen Plan depend on?
   a. Rapid movement through Belgium.
   b. A quick defeat of Russia.
   c. Invasion of England across the English Channel.
   d. Defeat of the British navy on the high seas.

10. What Turkish officer gained prominence when he rallied his soldiers on the heights of Gallipoli?
   a. Paul von Hindenburg.
   b. Erich Ludendorff.
   c. Shaw Mohammed Riza.
   d. Mutafa Kemal.

11. Where did troops who fought in World War I generally live along the Western Front?
   a. In concrete barracks built close to the front lines.
   b. In trenched dug into the ground.
   c. In tents pitched in campgrounds behind the front lines.
   d. In rented rooms in French villages.

12. How many soldiers were killed in the battle of Verdun?
   a. 100,000.
   b. 200,000.
   c. 500,000.
   d. 700,000

13. By the end of 1916, how many casualties had France suffered in World War I?
   a. 1 million.
   b. Two million.
   c. More than 31/2 million.
   d. Over 51/2 million.

14. Land that lay between the two sides during World War I was called?
   a. No man's land.
   b. The neutral zone.
   c. The twilight zone.
   d. The dark and bloody ground.

15. What does the term total war mean?
    a. Governments organized industries, economies, and public opinion in warring nations.
    b. All people in a country are destroyed.
    c. Total destruction of a nation occurs.
    d. All industry in a nation is destroyed.

16. What change in the lives of women occurred during World War I?
    a. Women were drafted into the military for the first time.
    b. Women were sent to the front lines to fight in a war for the first time.
    c. More Women entered the workforce to support their families.
    d. Women began to march in protest of going to war in 1914.

17. According to estimates, how many German civilians starved to death during WWI?
    a. 50,000.
    b. 100,000.
    c. 500,000.
    d. 750,000.

18. How did Irish nationalists see England's struggle against Germany?
    a. As an opportunity to win independence from England.
    b. As an opportunity to prove their loyalty to England.
    c. The Irish were pretty indifferent during the conflict.
    d. The Irish strongly supported the English.

19. After the March Revolution in Russia, who was chosen to head the Provisional Government as prime minister?
    a. Leon Trotsky
    b. Vladimir Lenin
    c. Alexander Kerensky
    d. Joseph Stalin

20. Who led the Bolshevik Revolution in Russia?
    a. Alexander Kerensky
    b. Vladimir Lenin
    c. Leon Petrograd
    d. Josef Benski

21. When World War I broke out, which of the following best describes America's official position?
    a. America supported England.
    b. America supported Germany.
    c. Americans were neutral.
    d. Americans demanded that the League of Nations end the war as quickly as possible.

22. Which one of the following was part of Wilson's Fourteen Points?
    a. Allowing nations to negotiate secret treaties.
    b. Creating a League of Nations.
    c. Restoring the Austrian Empire in the Balkans.
    d. Doing away with self-determination.

23. Which one of the following was not a member of the Big Four?
    a. Woodrow Wilson.
    b. David Lloyd George.
    c. Georges Clemenceau.
    d. Paul von Hindenburg.

24. What did the war guilt clause included in the Treaty of Versailles do?
    a. Justified war reparations by forcing Germany to accept responsibility for the damages of World War I caused by the aggression of Germany.
    b. Set war reparations against Germany at 50 billion dollars.
    c. Blamed England for causing the War.
    d. Set no blame for the cause of World War I.

25. The Treaty of Versailles created resentments in Germany that
    a. Helped give rise to Adolph Hitler.
    b. Made Germany turn toward Russia as an natural ally.
    c. Made Germany turn toward Japan for help against France.
    d. Gave rise to a communist controlled government.

MATCHING: Match the response in column B with the item in column A.

Column A

_____ 1.   Francis Ferdinand
_____ 2.   Otto von Bismarck
_____ 3.   Triple Alliance
_____ 4.   Triple Entente
_____ 5.   Kaiser Wilhelm II
_____ 6.   Unrestricted Submarine Warfare
_____ 7.   Schlieffen Plan
_____ 8.   Battle of Tannenberg
_____ 9.   Battle of Gallipoli
_____ 10. Verdun
_____ 11. Somme
_____ 12. Georges Clemenceau
_____ 13. David Lloyd George
_____ 14. Nicholas II
_____ 15. Christmas Present
_____ 16. Passchendaele
_____ 17. Zepplin
_____ 18. *Britannia*
_____ 19. March Revolution
_____ 20. Bolshevik Revolution
_____ 21. Lenin
_____ 22. Treaty of Versailles
_____ 23. Fourteen Points
_____ 24. The Big Four
_____ 25. League of Nations

Column B

a. David Lloyd George, Vittorio Orlando, Georges Clemenceau, and Woodrow Wilson.
b. One of the worst battles of World War I. Over 1.2 million men were killed or wounded on both sides.
c. The French Premier who said "Home policy? I wage war! Foreign policy? I wage war! All the time I wage war!"
d. A German airship used in World War I.
e. The Austrian Archduke whose assassination triggered World War I.

128

f. Germany, Austria-Hungary, Bulgaria, and the Ottoman Empire.

g. The German monarch during World War I.

h. Woodrow Wilson's peace plan presented at the Versailles Peace Conference.

i. Germany's "Iron Chancellor" who was an exponent of realpolitik.

j. An international peacekeeping organization created by the Treaty of Versailles.

k. A suffrage paper published in England by the Pankhursts.

l. The English Prime Minister during World War I.

m. England, France, Russia, Serbia, Romania and Montenegro.

n. Leader of the Bolsheviks in Russia.

o. The last Russian Czar.

p. Site of a battle in which German forces crushed an entire Russian army.

q. The British capture of Jerusalem in December 1917.

r. The event that ended the Russian monarchy.

s. A tactic in which Germany used U-boats to attack passenger ships.

t. A battle in the British campaign to capture Constantinople and drive Turkey from the war.

u. A battle on the Western Front in which 700,000 men were killed or wounded.

v. An event that toppled the Provisional Government in Russia and brought the Communists to power.

w. A German military plan developed in 1905 that called for rapid movement into western France through Belgium.

x. The diplomatic agreement that ended World War I and created the League of Nations.

y. A four-month British offensive in Belgium in which the Allies suffered over 400,000 casualties and accomplished nothing of real significance.

ESSAY QUESTIONS: (Answer on separate paper)

1. Discuss the causes of World War I? Could the conflict have been prevented? Why or why not?

2. What role did women play in World War I?

3. Write an essay that discusses the major battles of World War I? Why could neither side make much progress?

4. Compare and contrast the war along the Western Front with that along the Eastern Front. Discuss the March Revolution and the Bolshevik Revolution in Russia.

ANSWERS TO CHAPTER TWENTY

TRUE/FALSE:

1-F; 2-T; 3-F; 4-F; 5-T; 6-T; 7-T; 8-F; 9-T; 10-F; 11-T; 12-T; 13-F; 14-F; 15-F; 16-T; 17-F; 18-T; 19-T; 20-F; 21-T; 22-F; 23-T; 24-T; 25-T

FILL-IN-THE-BLANKS:

1. Triple Alliance; 2. Triple Entente; 3. Sir Edward Gray; 4. Otto von Bismarck;
5. Entente Cordiale; 6. Ottoman Empire; 7. Alfred Nobel; 8. Black Hand;
9. Bethmann Hollweg; 10. Vittorio Orlando; 11. Georges Clemenceau;
12. Alexander Kerensky; 13. Rasputin; 14. Lusitania; 15. First Battle of the Marne;
16. Dinant; 17. Dreatnought; 18. Gavrilo Princip; 19. realpolitik; 20. Balance of Power;
21. General Joseph Joffre; 22. Winston Churchill; 23. Woodrow Wilson;
24. League of Nations; 25. Fourteen Points.

MULTIPLE CHOICE:

1-a; 2-c; 3-d; 4-b; 5-c; 6-a; 7-c; 8-b; 9-a; 10-d; 11-b; 12-d; 13-c; 14-a; 15-a; 16-c; 17-d; 18-a; 19-c; 20-b; 21-c; 22-b; 23-d; 24-a; 25-a

MATCHING:

1-e; 2-i; 3-f; 4-m; 5-g; 6-s; 7-w; 8-p; 9-t; 10-u; 11-b; 12-c; 13-l; 14-o; 15-q; 16-y; 17-d; 18-k; 19-r; 20-v; 21-n; 22-x; 23-h; 24-a; 25-j

CHAPTER TWENTY-ONE

THE INTERWAR ERA, 1920-1939

· ·

IDENTIFICATION: Briefly describe each term.

Weimer Republic

Adolf Hitler

Mein Kampf

Nazi

Fascism

German Workers Party

Dalmatia

Benito Mussolini

Alceste de Ambris

Filippe Marinetti

Giovanni Giolitti

Italo Balboa

Victor Emanuel III

Acerbo Election Law

Giacomo Mattcotti

War Guilt Clause

War Reparations Clause

Hermann Goring

Rudolf Hess

Alfred Rosenberg

SA (Sturmaliteiling)

Paul von Hindenburg

Third Reich

Hjalmar Sahacht

Autoliahn

Autarky

Alfonso XIII

General Miguel Primo de Rivera

Francisco Franco

Spanish Civil War

Vladimir Lenin

Russian Civil War

Red Russians

White Russians

Leon Trotsky

New Economic Policy

Joseph Stalin

Policy of Collectivization

Great Purge

Raymond Poincare

Edward Herriot

Ruhr Crisis

Rapallo Agreement

Logical Positivism

Max Weber

Carl Jung

Oswald Spengler

Erich Remarque

Jean-Paul Sartre

Existentialism

Otto Dix

Kathe Kollwitz

Expressionism

Walter Gropius

Great Depression

League of Nations

Mukden Incident

World Disarmament Conference

Stress Front

Ethiopia

Spanish Civil War

Pact of Steel

Tripartite Agreement

Munich Agreement

Appeasement

Nazi-Soviet Pact

TRUE/FALSE: Indicate whether each statement is true (T) or false (F). The correct answers are given at the end of the chapter.

———— 1. Germany's Weimar Republic was one of the most democratic governments in the world.

———— 2. During the period between the World Wars, Europe embraced both liberal and conservative political extremism.

———— 3. The interwar period witnessed heightened class conflict in many European countries.

———— 4. During the interwar period European nations, for the most part, restored the old political, economic, and social order that had existed prior to the outbreak of the First World War.

———— 5. Ethnic tensions largely subsided in most European nations during the interwar period.

———— 6. Fascism, in many respects, was a revolution against revolution as it was largely in opposition to socialist revolutions that swept European nations after World War I.

———— 7. Fascists in general were politically extremely conservative.

———— 8. Benito Mussolini ruled Fascist Italy as head of an elected parliamentary government after 1925.

———— 9. Adolf Hitler was able to impose Fascism on Germany due to political, economic, and social instability present after World War I.

———— 10. The Weimar Republic faced massive inflation following World War I.

———— 11. Lower and middle class people generally benefitted from the inflation that gripped Germany during the interwar period because they could easily pay mortgages and other loans.

———— 12. Adolf Hitler studied painting at the Vienna Academy of Fine Arts.

———— 13. Adolf Hitler and the Nazi Party substantially lowered unemployment after they came to power in Germany during the 1930s.

———— 14. Spain embraced communism during the interwar period.

———— 15. Russia, like Italy and Germany, became Fascist during the 1920s.

———— 16. Red forces won the Russian Civil War, defeating White Russians in 1922.

———— 17. Lenin's New Economic Policy allowed some private ownership of property.

———— 18. Joseph Stalin is generally regarded as a benevolent dictator.

———— 19. Russian peasants resisted Stalin's policy of collectivization.

———— 20. Russian women were given equal rights in the Communist U.S.S.R.

———— 21. France and England, like Germany and Italy, embraced Fascism during Europe's interwar period.

———— 22. World War I reinforced the European belief that human progress through science and technology was inevitable.

———— 23. Logical Positivists generally held that human emotion was nearly as important as scientific observation and mathematical principles in discovering reality.

———— 24. The Great Depression of the 1930s contributed to the rise of totalitarian governments in Europe.

———— 25. The League of Nations is generally regarded as an impotent institution.

FILL-IN-THE-BLANKS: Write the appropriate word(s) to complete the sentence. The correct answers are given at the end of the chapter.

1. —————————— resolved the Czechoslovakian Crisis by giving the Sudetenland to Germany and the Teschen Province to Poland.

2. —————————— , signed in September 1940, created a formal military alliance between Germany, Japan, and Italy. This treaty is often informally called the Axis Agreement.

3. —————————— won the Spanish Civil War when he defeated Republican forces in 1939.

4. England, France, and Italy formed the—————————— to keep an eye on Hitler's actions in the future.

5. The —————————— occurred on September 18, 1931 when a railroad track owned by Japan was blown up at Mukden, China.

6. —————————— , a German architect, was Europe's most important proponent of functional architecture.

7. —————————— was a school of art whose proponents maintained that art did not necessarily need to have a subject because color and line give painting form.

8. —————————— , in The Decline of the West and Hour of Decision, maintained that the masses were incapable of making informed decisions or electing capable leaders.

9. Bertrand Russell and others developed a set of fatalistic ideas called —————————— that held that life had little meaning and that it was useless for humans to think about the meaning of life.

10. In—————————— Max Weber argued that religion was an economic force that gave rise to world capitalism.

11. —————————— , negotiated in 1922 established a trade pact between Russia and Germany and allowed Germany to construct factories in the Soviet Union to produce military weapons.

12. —————————— occurred when France occupied a German industrial region when Germany was unable to make reparation payments.

13. _____ a ruthless dictator who ruled the Soviet Union with an iron hand and who ordered the execution of numerous Russians who resisted his reform.

14. _____ led the Bolsheviks when they overthrew Russia's provisional government during the First World War.

15. _____ led the Red Russian Forces during the Russian Civil War.

16._____ was a hated figure who, with the king's permission, controlled Spain through marital law decrees from 1923 to 1930.

17. The Weimar Republic president forced to name Adolf Hitler chancellor was_____ .

18. Adolf Hitler wrote a book titled_____ while imprisoned that expressed his hatred of Jews, Communists, Socialists, and liberals.

19. From 1918 until 1933 Germans lived under the_____ , a democratic government.

20. _____ was the Fascist dictator of Italy during the interwar period.

21. On October 27, 1922 Italy's Fascist leader ordered a_____ to rid the Italian capital of leftist officials.

22. _____ was the small political party Adolf Hitler turned into the Nazi Party.

23. Erich Remarque's novel_____ is perhaps the best anti-war novel produced in the aftermath of the First World War.

24._____ , a German veteran, produced paintings that focused on death and destruction.

25. Jean Paul Sartre developed the philosophy of_____ in his play No Exit.

MULTIPLE CHOICE: Circle the correct response. The correct answers are given at the end of the chapter.

1. Which of the following statements is accurate about the Weimar Republic?
    a. It was a ruthless dictatorship.
    b. Paul von Hindenburg was Communist.
    c. On paper, it was one of the most democratic governments in the world.
    d. It was Fascist and socialist together.

2. Which one of the following was not a ruling dynasty that fell as a result of World War I?
    a. The Hapsburgs.
    b. The Hohenzollern.
    c. The Romanovs.
    d. The Ottomans.

3. Which of the following statements is accurate?
    a. World War I had made the world safe for democracy.
    b. Italy, Germany, and Spain remained democracies throughout the interwar period.
    c. England, France, and the United States elected Fascist governments during the 1920s.
    d. Russia was controlled by a Communist dictatorship.

4. Why did Fascists gain a foothold in Italy following World War I?
    a. Because Italians were disillusioned due to several severe problems the country faced.
    b. Because Italians had been Fascist before the great war began.
    c. Because Italy did not have a tradition of democratic government.
    d. Because a Fascist government was imposed on Italy by the Treaty of Versailles.

5. What did the Acerbo Election Law do?
    a. Gave 2/3rds of the seats in the lower chamber of Italy's Parliament to the political party receiving the largest number of votes.
    b. Created a winner take all rule for electoral votes in Italy's presidential election.
    c. Made it impossible for Fascist to control Italy's government.
    d. Allowed the Nazi's to take control of Germany's government.

6. Why was Adolf Hitler able to impose Fascism on Germany?
    a. Because the Versailles Peace Treaty mandated that Germany have a Fascist regime.
    b. Because Germany faced much political, economic, and social instability following World War I.
    c. Because Paul von Hindenburg was secretly Fascist.
    d. Because the German people feared invasion from Russia.

7. What effect did the War Reparations clause in the Treaty of Versailles have on Germany?
    a. It strengthened Germany's economy during the 1920s.
    b. It enabled the Weimar Republic to survive.
    c. It created massive inflation that weakened the Weimar government and the German economy.
    d. It laid the foundation for a strong German economy.

8. By Christmas of 1923, how many German marks were equivalent to one American dollar?
    a. Five hundred thousand.
    b. One million.
    c. Two billion.
    d. Two trillion.

9. Which one of the following was not an associate of Adolf Hitler?
    a. Hermann Goring.
    b. Rudolf Hess.
    c. Alfred Rosenberg.
    d. Joseph Staling.

10. Nazi policies had what effect on Germany's economy during the 1930s?
    a. They produced the worst depression in German history.
    b. Caused German factories to run at full capacity.
    c. They produced a period of massive inflation that destroyed the middle class.
    d. Created massive unemployment.

11. Which one of the following did not occur during the interwar period?
    a. Adolf Hitler rose to power in Germany.
    b. Benito Mussolini imposed Fascism on Italy.
    c. Lenin took control of Russia during the Bolshevik Revolution.
    d. General Franco took power in Spain.

12. Which one of the following Nazi policies did not play a role in Germany's economic revival during the 1930s?
    a. Hitler spent millions on public infrastructure.
    b. Nazi officials instituted strict wage and price controls.
    c. Hitler took Germany out of the world banking and financial system.
    d. Hjalmar Schacht, Hitler's chief economic advisor, loosened the government's tight control of the economy to free up capital for needed investment.

13. What initiated the Spanish Civil War?
    a. Replacement of an elected government with a Fascist dictatorship.
    b. Abolition of the Catholic Church.
    c. Nationalization of private property.
    d. Election of a liberal democratic government.

14. Who led Red Russian forces in the Russian Civil War?
    a. Joseph Stalin.
    b. Vladimir Lenin.
    c. Leon Trotsky.
    d. Czar Nicholas II.

15. Which of the following was not a feature of Lenin's New Economic Policy?
    a. It prohibited all ownership of private property.
    b. It forbade corporations from selling stock.
    c. It permitted employers to pay wages to workers.
    d. It allowed farmers to sell crops in public markets.

16. What prompted the Ruhr Crisis?
    a. France seized German factories when a war reparation payment was missed.
    b. England's insistence that Germany repay loans made to German factories.
    c. The outbreak of the Spanish Civil War.
    d. Hyperinflation made it difficult for Germany to repay American Loans.

17. What did the Rapallo Treaty allow Germany to do in 1922?
    a. Allowed Germany to construct factories in Russia to build weapons in violation of the Versailles Peace Treaty.
    b. Established a trade pact between France and Germany.
    c. Trade with the United States.
    d. Form an alliance with Switzerland against the Soviet Union.

18. Which of the following statements is true about European culture and society during the interwar period?
    a. The European faith in progress became even greater.
    b. Europeans largely lost faith that science and technology would inevitably improve human life.
    c. Europeans fully adopted the idea of history as progress.
    d. Optimism permeated European society during the interwar period.

19. Rudolf Carnap belonged to which of the following?
   a. Existentialists.
   b. Logical Positivism.
   c. Neo-Nazis.
   d. Expressionism.

20. Jean-Paul Sartre was —————— .
   a. A Logical Positivist.
   b. A Neo-Nazi.
   c. An Existentialist.
   d. An Expressionist.

21. Erich Remarque is best known for ——————.
   a. Writing The Decline of the West.
   b. Writing The Hour of Decision.
   c. Writing All Quiet on the Western Front.
   d. Writing No Exit.

22. Architecture styles during Europe's interwar period
   a. Embraced emotion.
   b. Generally did not convey a building's purpose.
   c. Adorned buildings for the sake of beauty.
   d. Embraced the principle of functionality.

23. What did the English Parliament do to alleviate the impact of the Great Depression?
   a. Passed laws promoting free trade in 1932.
   b. Lowered England's protective tariffs.
   c. Allowed the minimum wage law to expire.
   d. Took England off the gold standard in 1931.

24. Which of the following is accurate?
   a. The United States joined the League of Nations during the 1930s.
   b. President Hoover rejected a plan that declared a moratorium on war debt payments.
   c. Japanese forces were driven out of Manchuria by German soldiers.
   d. International isolation within England, France, and the United States became more pronounced as a result of the Great Depression.

25. Neville Chamberlain's policy in which England and France agreed to allow Hitler and Germany to Czechoslovakian territory was called ——————.
   a. Appeasement.
   b. Bi-laterialism.
   c. The Dove Principle.
   d. Utilitarianism.

MATCHING: Match the response in column B with the item in column A.

Column A

———— 1. Edoward Daladier
———— 2. Sudetenland
———— 3. Kurt von Schuschnigg
———— 4. Albania
———— 5. Spanish Civil War
———— 6. Adolf Hitler
———— 7. League of Nations
———— 8. Great Depression
———— 9. Functionality
————10. Kathe Kollwitz
————11. No Exit
————12. Bertrand Russell
————13. Max Weber
————14. Vladimir Lenin
————15. Karl Marx
————16. Autarky
————17. S.A.
————18. Ruhr Crisis
————19. Weimar Republic
————20. Benito Mussolini
————21. Fascism
————22. Interwar Period
————23. Hapsburgs
————24. Romanovs
————25. Bolsheviks

Column B

a. The Austrian Chancellor forced to appoint several Nazis to critical cabinet positions.
b. Taken by Italy in 1939.
c. Style of architecture style in which a building's appearance showed its purpose.
d. A German artist whose work portrayed grief survivors felt for loved ones killed in the First World War.
e. A founder of Logical Positivism.
f. French leader at the Munich Conference.
g. German leader whose aggressive foreign policy led to the outbreak of World War II.
h. Leader of Russian Communists.
i. Territory Germany was given at the Munich Conference.
j. Conflict won by Fascists that was a dress rehearsal for World War II.
k. Policy designed by Hitler to make Germany economically self-sufficient.
l. World peace keeping agency.
m. Police force Hitler created to stifle opposition.
n. Economic downturn that stressed national economies prior to World War II.
o. Play written by Jean-Paul Sartre.
p. Right wing conservative governmental philosophy that produced European dictators.
q. Name given to Russian Communists.
r. Wrote The Protestant Ethic and The Spirit of Capitalism.
s. Austrian ruling dynasty.
t. Wrote The Communist Manifesto.
u. Germany's democratic government after World War I.
v. Italian dictator.
w. The time between the World Wars.
x. Russian ruling dynasty.
y. Prompted by French invasions of German industrial region.

ESSAY QUESTIONS: (Answer on separate paper)

1. Discuss events that occurred throughout Europe during the interwar period that led to the outbreak of the Second World War.
2. Write a well developed essay that discusses European culture and society during the interwar period. Pay particular attention to changes that took place after World War I.
3. Compare and contrast Fascism as it existed in Italy, Germany, and Spain with Communism in the Soviet Union.
4. Analyze the various factors that gave rise to totalitarianism in various European nations.
5. Write an essay that analyzes whether the western democracies could have prevented World War II.

ANSWERS TO CHAPTER TWENTY-ONE

TRUE/FALSE:

1-T; 2-T; 3-T; 4-F; 5-F; 6-T; 7-T; 8-F; 9-T; 10-T; 11-F; 12-F; 13-T; 14-F; 15-F; 16-T; 17-T; 18-F; 19-T; 20-T; 21-F; 22-F; 23-F; 24-T; 25-T

FILL-IN-THE-BLANKS:

1. Munich; 2. Tripartite Agreement; 3. General Francisco Franco; 4. Stressa Front;
5. The Manchurian Incident; 6. Walter Gropius; 7. Expressionism; 8. Oswald Spengler;
9. Logical Positivism' 10. The Protestant Ethic and the Spirit of Capitalism;
11. Rapallo Agreement; 12. The Ruhr Crisis; 13. Joseph Stalin; 14. Vladimir Lenin;
15. Leon Trotsky; 16. General Miguel Primo de Rivera; 17. Paul von Hindenburg;
18. Mein Kampf; 19. Weimar Republic; 20. Benito Mussolini; 21. March on Rome;
22. German Workers Party; 23. All Quiet on the Western Front; 24. Otto Dix;
25. Existentialism

MULTIPLE CHOICE:

1-c; 2-d; 3-d; 4-a; 5-a; 6-b; 7-c; 8-d; 9-d; 10-b; 11-c; 12-d; 13-a; 14-c; 15-a; 16-a; 17-a; 18-b; 19-b; 20-c; 21-c; 22-d; 23-d; 24-d; 25-a

MATCHING:

1-f; 2-i; 3-a; 4-b; 5-j; 6-g; 7-l; 8-n; 9-c; 10-d; 11-o; 12-e; 13-r; 14-h; 15-t; 16-k; 17-m; 18-y; 19-u; 20-v; 21-p; 22-w; 23-s; 24-x; 25-q

CHAPTER TWENTY-TWO

WORLD WAR II 1939-1945

IDENTIFICATION: Briefly describe each term.

Winston Churchill

Blitzkrieg

Ardennes Forest

Sitzkrieg

Charles deGaulle

Dunkirk

Sedan

Vicky France

Operation Sea Lion

Franklin Roosevelt

D-Day

Island-hopping

Douglas MacArthur

Dwight David Eisenhower

George Patton

Luftwaffe

Battle of Britain

Soft Underbelly

Erwin Rommel

Afrika Korps

Bernard Montgomery

London Blitz

Operation Barbarossa

Benito Mussolini

Stalingrad

Scorched Earth Policy

Operation Torch

Midway

Pearl Harbor

Coral Sea

Iwo Jima

Royal Air Force

Warsaw Uprising

Battle of the Bulge

Battle of Leyte Gulf

Kamikaze

Hiroshima

Nagasaki

Atomic bomb

Manhattan Project

Submarines

Battle of the Atlantic

The Big Three

Joseph Stalin

Atlantic Charter

Yalta Agreement

United Nations

Casablanca Conference

Harry Truman

Adolf Hitler

Potsdam Conference

Unconditional surrender

Trident Summit

Teheran Conference

Nuremberg Trials

Executive Order 9066

Curtis LeMay

Treblinka

Holocaust

Extermination Camps

Warsaw Ghetto

Neville Chamberlain

TRUE/FALSE: Indicate whether each statement is true (T) or false (F). The correct answers are given at the end of the chapter.

———— 1. World War II involved three sets of shifting alliances.

———— 2. One cause of World War II was that many Germans did not feel that they had really lost the First World War.

————3. World War II can be divided into three basic phrases.

———— 4. The forces rescued at Dunkirk were essentially all the army England had at the time.

———— 5. Germany won the Battle of Britain, a key to German success early in the Second World War.

———— 6. Benito Mussolini was the leader of the Soviet Union during World War II.

———— 7. Stalin, Roosevelt, and Churchill are often called the Big Three during World War II.

———— 8. 1942 was the pivotal year of decision during World War II.

———— 9. The Japanese attack on Pearl Harbor caught American forces off guard.

———— 10. The Russian Winter had little impact on the German defeat during the Second World War.

————11. American general George S. Patton was made supreme commander in the European Theater of War.

———— 12. May 8, 1945 is known as V-E Day.

———— 13. The first American atomic bomb was dropped on the Japanese city of Nagasaki.

———— 14. Roosevelt, Churchill, and Stalin met at the Casablanca Conference.

———— 15. Roosevelt and Churchill made the decision to invade France in the Spring of 1944 at the Quadrant Conference in Quebec.

———— 16. Franklin Roosevelt was in ill health at the Yalta Conference.

_____ 17. The final wartime conference between the Big Three occurred at Potsdam in July 1945.

_____ 18. The Second World War is not generally considered a total war.

_____ 19. The accuracy of bombing in hitting strategically important targets during World War II was generally good.

_____ 20. Hitler's New Order was based on the idea that certain ethnic groups were superior to others and thus should rule over inferior peoples.

_____ 21. In all, the Nazis exterminated eleven million people during World War II.

_____ 22. Germany refused to use conquered people as slaves in Europe.

_____ 23. Civilian areas were often hit by airplanes during World War II.

_____ 24. Russian women served in combat roles to save their country during World War II.

_____ 25. The decision to drop the atomic bomb on the Japanese city of Hiroshima was made by President Truman at the Yalta Conference.

FILL-IN-THE-BLANKS: Write the appropriate word(s) to complete the sentence. The correct answers are given at the end of the chapter.

1. _____ was the name given to the military alliance of Germany, Japan, and Italy during World War II.

2. _____ was the name given to the coordinated use of air attacks, tank warfare, and infantry in battle during World War II.

3. Russian efforts to take territory from Finland during World War II was called the _____.

4. The major German attack on France in 1940 came through the _____ region of Belgium.

5. _____ was the location at which German troops broke French lines on May 14, 1940.

153

6. Including Jews, Gypsies, homosexuals, and Slavs, the Nazis exterminated about
——————————————people during World War II.

7. ——————————————is the name given to the Nazi attempt to exterminate the world's
Jewish population.

8. The Nazis called their attempt to exterminate Europe's Jews the —————————— or Final
Solution.

9. —————————————— was the name given to Hitler's plan to make Germany ruler of the
world and using or exterminating other ethnic groups according to Nazi needs.

10. —————————————— was the German leader whose aggression was the primary cause of
World War II.

11.—————————————was a new weapon of mass destruction the United States developed in
the Manhattan Project.

12.—————————————was the American general who developed the strategy of Island-hopping to defeat Japanese forces in the Pacific Theater of Operations.

13.—————————————was the Allied strategy in which Nazi forces were attacked in southern
Europe because they were weakest there.

14. The American and English invasion of Normandy, France on June 6, 1944 is known as
————————————— .

15.—————————————was the supreme American commander in the European Theater of
Operations during World War II.

16.————————————— and —————————————were the two Japanese cities hit with
American atomic bombs in August 1945.

17.————————————— was a pledge by the United States and England to restore democracy
to all areas of Europe occupied by Nazi forces after World War II.

18.————————————— was the name given to the French government that collaborated with
the Nazis.

19. _____ was a May 1943 meeting between Roosevelt and Churchill in which plans for the invasion of Italy and D-Day were finalized.

20. The Battle of _____ in which American forces destroyed Japanese aircraft carriers in June 1942 represents the major turning point in the Pacific Theater during World War II.

21. _____ issued by President Roosevelt in February 1942, allowed American officials to round up and detain Japanese-Americans living on the West Coast.

22. _____ was the German admiral who developed the wolf-pact tactic used by German submarines during World War II.

23. _____ was the famed German commander of the Afrika Korps.

24. _____ was a massive German battleship sunk in May 1941 by the British navy.

25. _____ was used by Japanese forces to attack American ships due to a shortage of fuel and trained pilots.

MULTIPLE CHOICE: Circle the correct response. The correct answers are given at the end of the chapter.

1. Which of the following events happened first?
   a. Atomic bombs were dropped on Japan.
   b. Operation Barbarossa.
   c. The Allies invaded Italy.
   d. Germany invaded Denmark and Norway.

2. Which Japanese city was hit first by an atomic bomb in August 1945?
   a. Nagasaki.
   b. Tokyo.
   c. Edo.
   d. Hiroshima.

3. Which of the following statements best characterizes the first phase of World War II?
   a. From September 1939 through December 1941 Germany experienced spectacular combat success.
   b. A series of developments in Russia, North Africa, and the Pacific turned the war in favor of the Allies.
   c. The Allies slowly but steadily beat back Axis forces in all theaters of the war.
   d. Axis forces developed new weapons, including the jet fighter and nuclear missiles that were deployed against Allied forces in the European theatre.

4. Which of the following was not a turning point in favor of Allied forces during World War II?
   a. Stalingrad.
   b. Midway.
   c. The Sitzkrieg.
   d. The Battle of Britain.

5. Who was the British commander who turned the tide of war in North Africa with a victory over German forces at El Alamein?
   a. George S. Patton.
   b. Bernard Montgomery.
   c. Harold Alexander.
   d. Dwight David Eisenhower.

6. Which one of the following was not a cause of the Second World War?
   a. The League of Nations failed to stop Nazi aggression.
   b. The western democracies refused to appease German demands.
   c. Hitler and the Nazi government he headed wanted to use violence to overturn the Treaty of Versailles.
   d. The Bolsheviks rise to power in Russia created sufficient distrust and fear to make Fascism acceptable to some western democracies.

7. Although the total casualty figures for World War II can never be fully known, estimates place the number of civilian deaths at approximately
   a. 18 million.
   b. 30 million.
   c. 15 million.
   d. 10 million.

8. Approximately how many Gypsies did the Nazis exterminate?
   a. 250,000.
   b. 2 million.
   c. 5 million.
   d. 6 million.

9. What does the term "Holocaust" mean?
   a. Extermination by gas.
   b. Mass or complete sacrifice by fire.
   c. Death by the hand of God.
   d. Execution by legal means.

10. Under Hitler's New Order, which nation would rule all of Europe?
    a. England.
    b. Russia.
    c. Germany.
    d. Spain.

11. Which one of the following was not a primary element of the New Order?
    a. Plunder.
    b. Slavery.
    c. Endlosung.
    d. World Peace.

12. The Blitzkrieg
    a. Was used first when Germany invaded England.
    b. Involved the coordinated use of air power, tank attacks, and infantry.
    c. Made use of trench warfare.
    d. Relied upon naval vessels such as submarines to support infantry.

13. The Sitzkrieg refers to
    a. Inactivity on the Western Front during the first days of World War II.
    b. A new style of war Germany developed to avoid the trench warfare of the First World War.
    c. A type of fighting in which infantry could not advance with strategic support from artillery.
    d. The strategic placement of big guns to do the most damage to enemy cities.

14. Who replaced Neville Chamberlain as the British Prime Minister?
    a. Franklin Roosevelt.
    b. Winston Churchill.
    c. Harry Truman.
    d. Bernard Montgomery.

15. The United States, England, and Russia were called
    a. The Axis Alliance.
    b. The Grand Alliance.
    c. The Triple Entente.
    d. The Western Alliance.

16. Operation Overload
    a. Was the German invasion of Italy.
    b. Was commanded by Douglas MacArthur.
    c. Was Patton's invasion of North Africa.
    d. Was the Allied invasion of France in June 1944.

17. Which of the following is not a reason for England's victory over Germany in the Battle of Britain?
    a. England got support from the Russian Air Force.
    b. England produced more and better aircraft than did Germany.
    c. England used radar to direct British planes to critical locations.
    d. The ULTRA project gave England an advantage.

18. The Battle of the Bulge
    a. Was the last battle of the Pacific campaign.
    b. Was a German offensive in the Ardennes forest of Belgium.
    c. Was an Italian campaign in Sicily.
    d. Was the first battle fought in the campaign to drive German forces out of North Africa.

19. The country with the highest death toll in World War II was
    a. The United States.
    b. Germany.
    c. England.
    d. The Soviet Union.

20. World War II ended in the Pacific
    a. After the U.S. destroyed Japanese aircraft carriers at the Battle of Midway.
    b. After Americans invaded the Japanese home islands.
    c. After the U.S. dropped atomic bombs on Hiroshima and Nagasaki.
    d. After American forces firebombed Tokyo, the Japanese capital city.

21. At Katyn Forest in 1940
    a. Germany initiated the Holocaust.
    b. Russians killed about 12,000 Polish officers captured during the war.
    c. Polish forces defeated German and Russian forces.
    d. Germany executed the Polish president.

22. Dunkirk is best remembered for
    a. The German defeat of American forces.
    b. Being the turning point in the Pacific War.
    c. The end of Mussolini's rule in Italy.
    d. The heroic evacuation of British and French troops by boat.

23. Where did the final conference of the Big Three take place during World War II?
    a. Potsdam.
    b. Yalta.
    c. Stalingrad.
    d. Tehran.

24. Which agreement in 1941 contained a self-determination principle?
    a. The Yalta Agreement.
    b. The Nazi-Soviet Pact.
    c. The Atlantic Charter.
    d. The Treblanka Accord.

25. How many Americans died at Iwo Jima?
    a. 6821.
    b. 9492.
    c. 10,201.
    d. 15,634.

MATCHING: Match the response in column B with the item in column A.

COLUMN A
___ 1. Dwight David Eisenhower.
___ 2. Douglas MacArthur.
___ 3. ULTRA.
___ 4. Hiroshima.
___ 5. Nagasaki.
___ 6. Afrika Corps
___ 7. Final Solution.
___ 8. Battle of Britain.
___ 9. Soft Underbelly.
___ 10. Bernard Montgomery.
___ 11. George Patton.
___ 12. D-Day.
___ 13. Midway.
___ 14. United Nations.
___ 15. Dunkirk.
___ 16. The Grand Alliance.
___ 17. The Axis Powers.
___ 18. Charles DeGaulle.
___ 19. Winston Churchill.
___ 20. Operation Torch.
___ 21. Yalta.
___ 22. Potsdam.
___ 23. Luftwaffe.
___ 24. Harry Truman.
___ 25. Franklin Roosevelt.

COLUMN B
a. American President during most of World War II.
b. Commander of American forces in the Pacific.
c. Allied invasion of Normandy on June 6, 1944.
d. Second Japanese city hit by an atomic bomb.
e. American President who made the decision to drop atomic bombs on Japan.
f. Meeting of Allied leaders on Russian territory.
g. Germany, Italy, and Japan.
h. Supreme American commander in European Theatre.
i. First Japanese city destroyed by an atomic bomb.

j. Germany army commanded by Erwin Rommel.

k. Leader of French resistance during World War II.

l. Pacific battle in which Americans destroyed Japan's aircraft carriers.

m. Fought for control of English Channel.

n. Controversial British commander during World War II.

o. Site where British and French troops were evacuated by boat.

p. The German airforce.

q. British Prime Minister.

r. International peace keeping organization created after World War II.

s. Controversial American commander during World War II.

t. American and British strategy to attack German forces where they were weakest in southern Europe.

u. Meeting at which Truman received word of the successful testing of the atomic bomb.

v. Hitler's plan to exterminate European Jews.

w. The United States, the Soviet Union, and England.

x. U.S.-British landings on the eastern end of North Africa.

y. British project that broke German code using a captured German device.

ESSAY QUESTIONS: (Answer on separate paper)

1. Discuss the origins of World War II. Pay attention to specific events that led to the outbreak of war.

2. Identify the most important reasons the Allies won World War II.

3. Discuss the role technology played in World War II.

4. How important was naval warfare in the Second World War? Explain using specific events and developments along with historical evidence to support your answer.

5. Identify the most important diplomatic decisions made during World War II. Justify your choices with the use of historical evidence.

6. Describe the Nazi extermination of various groups throughout Europe. Could the Allies have prevented these exterminations? Explain.

7. Discuss the tensions between the U.S., England, and the Soviet Union during World War II/ What could have been done to ease those tensions?

ANSWERS TO CHAPTER TWENTY-TWO

TRUE/FALSE:

1.F; 2.T; 3.T; 4.T; 5.F; 6.F; 7.T; 8.T; 9.T; 10.F; 11.F; 12.T; 13.F; 14.F; 15.T; 16.T; 17.T; 18.F; 19.F; 20.T; 21.T; 22.F; 23.T; 24.T; 25.F

FILL-IN-THE-BLANKS:

1. Axis; 2. Blitzkrieg; 3. Winter War; 4. Ardennes; 5. Sedan; 6. 11 million; 7. Holocaust;
8. Endlosung; 9. New Order; 10. Adolf Hitler; 11. Atomic bomb; 12. MacArthur;
13. Soft Underbelly; 14. D-Day; 15. Eisenhower; 16. Hiroshima and Nagasaki;
17. Atlantic Charter; 18. Vicky Lane; 19. Trident Summit; 20. Midway;
21. Executive Order 9066; 22. Karl Donitz; 23. Erwin Rommel; 24. Bismarck; 25. Kamekaze

MULTIPLE CHOICE:

1.d; 2.d; 3.a; 4.c; 5.b; 6.b; 7.a; 8.a; 9.b; 10.c; 11.d; 12.b; 13.a; 14.b; 15.b; 16.d; 17.a; 18.b;19.d; 20.c; 21.b; 22.d; 23.a; 24.c; 25.a

MATCHING:

1.h; 2.b; 3.y; 4.i; 5.d; 6.j; 7.v; 8.m; 9.t; 10.n; 11.s; 12.c; 13. L; 14.r; 15.o; 16.w; 17.g; 18.h; 19.q; 20.x; 21.f; 22.u; 23.p; 24.e; 25.a

CHAPTER TWENTY-THREE

THE POSTWAR ERA 1945-1968

IDENTIFICATION: Briefly describe each term.

Iron Curtain

Cold War

Division of Europe

Azerbaijan

Lesson of Munich

Truman Doctrine

Containment

NATO

European Recovery Program

Warsaw Pact

MAD

Superpowers

ICBM

Berlin Crisis (1948-1949)

Cuban Missile Crisis

Fidel Castro

Bay of Pigs

Cold War Conflicts

Ho Chi Minh

Charles de Gaulle

Mahatma Gandhi

Arab-Israeli Wars

Suez Crisis

Josip Tito

COMECON

Stalinization

Nikita Khruschev

Hungarian Revolt

Berlin Wall

"Prague Spring"

Brezhnev Doctrine

Peaceful Coexistence

Nuremberg Trials

Konrad Adenauer

French Fifth Republic

Social Welfare State

European Coal and Steel Community

Common Market

Korean War

United Nations

Bretton Woods Conference

World Bank

GATT

Existentialism

Jean-Paul Sartre

Neo-Marxism

First, Second, and Third Worlds

Demotic Times

Age of Science

Mass Consumption

Nationalist Backlash

Women's Movement

Civil Rights Movement

Social Welfare State

Environmental Movement

War on Poverty

TRUE/FALSE: Indicate whether each statement is true (T) or false (F). The correct answers are given at the end of the chapter.

____ 1. After World War II Europe lost its dominant position in world affairs.

____ 2. The Cold War was fueled by competition between the U.S. and the Soviet Union.

____ 3. Communist candidates did very well in the Austrian elections of 1945.

____ 4. The Truman Doctrine promised American aid to countries facing Communist-sponsored revolts.

____ 5. George Kennan originated the idea of "containment."

____ 6. An ICBM is a missile that can carry nuclear warheads.

____ 7. The "MAD" doctrine made direct war between the U.S. and U.S.S.R. more likely.

____ 8. The Cuban Missile Crisis was resolved by negotiation.

____ 9. Europe was divided between areas of American and German influence.

____ 10. Most European-controlled colonies gained their independence in the postwar era.

____ 11. The United Nations created a Jewish state but not an Arab one in Palestine.

____ 12. COMECON was set up to send Soviet aid to Eastern Europe.

____ 13. The Soviet Red Army crushed the Hungarian Revolt in 1956.

____ 14. The Berlin Wall was built to keep East Germans from fleeing to West Germany.

____ 15. The Soviet Union enjoyed excellent economic growth during the Brezhnev years.

____ 16. West Germany suffered from political instability and economic failure during the 1950s and 1960s.

____ 17. Charles de Gaulle restored stability to France in the Fifth Republic.

____ 18. There was more government intervention in society and the economy in European social welfare states than in the USA.

____ 19. The United Nations Security Council had the authority to order military actions.

____ 20. The Bretton Woods Conference failed to improve economic cooperation.

____ 21. The Communist Party gained popularity in France and Italy in the postwar years.

____ 22. Improvements in living standards were strongly related to government-funded scientific research.

____ 23. Beginning in the 1960s, Western families tended to become larger.

____ 24. The Women's, Civil Rights, and Environmental Movements challenged many traditional beliefs in Western culture.

____ 25. Most Western governments provided increased social services for citizens during the postwar period.

FILL-IN-THE-BLANKS: Write the appropriate word(s) to complete the sentence. The correct answers are given at the end of the chapter.

1. _____ surrendered on May 7, 1945, ending World War II in Europe.

2. _____was a U. S. policy to provide aid to anti-Communist governments.

3. _____was an Eastern European country that avoided direct Soviet control.

4. _____was the Soviet dictator who imposed Communism in Eastern Europe.

5. _____was the city blockaded by the Soviets in an attempt to starve it into surrender.

6. _____, the "crown jewel" of Britain's empire, became independent in 1947.

7. _____was the first customs union between cooperating European countries.

8. _____political parties were primarily Catholic and favored European integration.

9. _____drew U. S. and U. N. forces into Asian conflict from 1950 to 1953.

10. _____were held to judge the crimes of Nazi leaders.

11. _____was the military alliance formed between the Soviet Union and its East European allies.

12. _____tried to implement reforms in Poland in 1956 until Soviet troops intervened.

13. _____of Hungary was overthrown by Red Army troops in 1956 and later executed.

14. _____, an Arab nationalist, nationalized the Suez Canal. His country was invaded by Britain, France, and Israel during the Suez Crisis.

15. _____was recalled to power in France in 1958 to resolve the Algerian Crisis.

16. _____proclaimed U. S. solidarity with Western Europe by saying, "Ich bin ein Berliner."

17. _____ordered construction of the Berlin Wall in 1961.

18. _____doctrine held that there would be no winners in a nuclear war.

19. _____was the closest the Cold War superpowers ever came to direct war.

20. _____countries enjoyed the highest standard of living in world history.

21. _____replaced competition between countries in European economics.

22. _____was a theory that blamed the former imperialist industrial nations for most of the problems in the poorer nations.

23. _____became the world's new lingua franca.

24. _____withdrew from the NATO command in 1966. This nation wished to assert more of its own authority and believed American influence over Western Europe had grown too strong.

25. _____was led in the U. S. by figures such as Martin Luther King, Jr. and Malcolm X.

MULTIPLE CHOICE: Circle the correct response. The correct answers are given at the end of the chapter.

1. What was the condition of Europe at the end of World War II in 1945?
   a. Europe retained most of its wealth and influence.
   b. The defeated nations, Germany and Italy, were the only ones seriously damaged.
   c. Most European countries were devastated and bankrupt.
   d. Western Europe was prospering but Eastern Europe was impoverished.

2. The world's most influential countries from 1945 to 1991 were
   a. The United States and the Union of soviet Socialist Republics
   b. China and Japan
   c. Great Britain, Germany, and France
   d. The United States and Germany

3. Which of the following was not a cause of the Cold War rivalry?
   a. political philosophy
   b. economic philosophy
   c. strategic military considerations
   d. racial prejudice

4. Describe the Stalinization of Eastern Europe.
   a. It was a policy of harsh rule to enforce Communism and repress nationalism.
   b. Stalinization was an economic policy designed to provide jobs.
   c. It was an attempt to restore greater personal liberty.
   d. Stalinization was a program of defensive military preparedness.

5. Which American president first adopted the policy of containment to resist suspected Soviet aggression?
   a. Franklin D. Roosevelt
   b. Harry S Truman
   c. Dwight D. Eisenhower
   d. John F. Kennedy

6. What U. S. aid program sent billions of dollars to Western Europe to promote its postwar recovery?
   a. GATT
   b. Marshall Plan
   c. Truman Doctrine
   d. Peace Corps

7. What is the most likely reason the U. S. and U. S. S. R. avoided a full-scale war between them?
   a. Memories of their wartime alliance against Hitler
   b. The presence of Russian immigrants in the United States
   c. The ECSC
   d. The MAD doctrine

8. Benelux, ECSC, and EEC are all examples of
   a. Cold War military alliances
   b. European economic integration
   c. United Nations relief agencies
   d. Soviet missile systems

9. Rather than attacking each other directly, the U. S. and U. S. S. R. most often competed for influence in the
   a. First World
   b. Second World
   c. Third World
   d. League of Nations

10. Which of these former European colonies gained its independence peacefully?
    a. Indonesia
    b. Vietnam
    c. Nigeria
    d. Algeria

11. What was the result when Nikita Khruschev relaxed Soviet rule in Eastern Europe?
    a. Nationalist defiance and anti-Soviet rebellions broke out.
    b. Eastern Europeans renewed their loyalty to the Soviets.
    c. Economic growth greatly improved.
    d. The U. S. S. R. became more democratic.

12. What two powerful military alliances confronted each other in Central Europe during the Cold War?
    a. Allies and Axis
    b. NATO and Warsaw Pact
    c. SEATO and UNESCO
    d. Israel and the Arab League

13. According to the text, how successful was the United Nations in preventing conflict and war?
    a. Not very effective
    b. Somewhat effective
    c. Moderately effective
    d. Highly effective

14. The Berlin Wall was built to
    a. protect East Berlin from NATO attack
    b. prevent West Berliners from escaping to the East
    c. protect West Berlin from Communism
    d. prevent East Berliners from escaping to the West

15. Describe Western European economic growth in the 1950s and 1960s.
    a. Growth was slow and the region remained in poverty.
    b. France and Britain recovered but Germany remained poor.
    c. There were good and bad periods. Overall growth was average.
    d. Growth was outstanding during these decades.

16. Describe Soviet and East European economic growth in the 1950s and 1960s.
    a. There was no economic improvement in Eastern Europe during this period.
    b. At first there was good growth, but it stalled in the 1960s.
    c. Growth enjoyed a small but steady increase during these years.
    d. Soviet and East European economies were the best in the world by the end of this period.

17. What did the outcomes of the Hungarian Revolt and the Prague Spring show?
    a. Eastern Europeans did not care about political matters.
    b. The Soviet Union would use military power to enforce its form of Communism in Eastern Europe.
    c. The Soviets lacked the power to keep Eastern Europe under their control.
    d. The Hungarian and Czech people supported the Communist system.

18. What were the "three miracles" of Western European recovery?
    a. colonial empire, economic integration, and the rule of law
    b. economic recovery, military power, and cultural unification
    c. economic recovery, political integration, and cultural unification
    d. democratic election, military power, and the Prague Spring

19. The Brezhnev era in the Soviet Union was characterized by
    a. stagnation, corruption, and decay
    b. a return to the terror of the Stalinist era
    c. the relaxation of government controls
    d. a new sense of dynamism and progress

20. Which of these four U. S. goals achieved the least success?
    a. strong U. S. economic growth
    b. the recovery of Western Europe
    c. a strong and effective United Nations organization
    d. a stable world financial system

21. The International Bank for Reconstruction and Development (World Bank) provided funds for economic projects in
    a. newly independent third-world countries
    b. North America
    c. Communist countries
    d. China and Japan

22. Where did neo-Marxists place the blame for Europe's twentieth century problems?
    a. the Fascist powers of World War II
    b. monarchs and upper class aristocrats
    c. labor unions and their working class members
    d. middle class values and American materialism

23. Wars were fought between Communists and anti-Communists in all of the following <u>except</u>
    a. Vietnam
    b. India
    c. Greece
    d. Korea

24. According to the text, how did Western economic systems compare from 1946-1968?
    a. The American laissez-faire system was superior to the European mixed economy.
    b. The European mixed economy was superior to American laissez-faire.
    c. Both systems produced excellent results.
    d. Both systems were failures.

25. By 1968 what was the status of European economic and political integration?
    a. full integration
    b. partial integration
    c. minimal integration
    d. no integration

MATCHING: Match the response in column B with the item in column A.

Column A

_____1. German couple who lived through Europe's transformation.
_____2. Greatest world power after World War II.
_____3. Economic system of the Soviet Union.
_____4. Statesman who described the East-West division of Europe as an "iron curtain."
_____5. Last leader of the U.S.S.R.
_____6. U.S. belief that appeasement leads to war.
_____7. Anti-Soviet military alliance.
_____8. American aid program for Europe.
_____9. The Bay of Pigs invasion was intended to overthrow him.
_____10. Leader of Vietnamese opposition to French rule.
_____11. Nationalists favoring a Jewish state in Palestine.

_____12. Postwar repression of Eastern Europe.
_____13. Policy of military intervention to defend pro-Soviet regimes.
_____14. He was removed from Soviet leadership in 1964.
_____15. Conservative Soviet leader whose economic policies failed.
_____16. Chancellor who presided over West German recovery.
_____17. Political/economic system in postwar Western Europe.
_____18. Concept of Western political cooperation.
_____19. European Economic Community
_____20. It lowered global trade barriers.
_____21. Existentialist philosopher.
_____22. Poor countries, mostly former colonies.
_____23. International lingua franca.
_____24. Movement questioning belief in the superiority of Western attitudes.
_____25. Government committed to a rising standard of living for all its citizens.

Column B

a. Winston Churchill
b. Third World
c. Social welfare state
d. Nikita Khruschev
e. Hans and Helga Schmidt
f. Common Market
g. NATO
h. Cultural relativism
i. Ho Chi Minh
j. United States
k. Liberal democratic capitalism
l. English
m. Konrad Adenauer
n. Fidel Castro
o. Communism
p. Marshall Plan
q. Mikhail Gorbachev
r. Brezhnev Doctrine
s. Lesson of Munich
t. Jean-Paul Sartre
u. European federalism
v. Zionists
w. GATT
x. Stalinization
y. Leonid Brezhnev

ESSAY QUESTIONS: (Answer on separate paper)

1. What factors explain Western Europe's strong economic recovery in the two decades following World War II? Which factor do you feel was the most important? Why?
2. Was the Cold War inevitable? If so, why? If not, tell how it could have been averted.
3. What factors were propelling Europe toward closer integration in the postwar years? What factors were driving Europe apart?
4. How did third-world nationalism affect the colonial empires of the European powers? In what ways did it become part of the Cold War struggle?

ANSWERS TO CHAPTER TWENTY-THREE

TRUE/FALSE:

1-T, 2-T, 3-F, 4-T, 5-T, 6-T, 7-F, 8-T, 9-F, 10-T, 11-F, 12-F, 13-T, 14-T, 15-F, 16-F, 17-T, 18-T, 19-T, 20-F, 21-T, 22-T, 23-F, 24-T, 25-T

FILL-IN-THE-BLANKS:

1. Nazi Germany, 2. Truman Doctrine, 3. Yugoslavia, 4. Josef Stalin, 5. West Berlin,
6. India, 7. BENELUX, 8. Christian Democratic, 9. Korean War, 10. Nuremberg Trials,
11. Warsaw Pact, 12. Wladislaw Gomulka , 13. Imre Nagy, 14. Gamel Abdel Nasser,
15. Charles De Gaulle, 16. John F. Kennedy, 17. Nikita Khruschev, 18. MAD,
19. Cuban Missile Crisis, 20. Western capitalist, 21. Cooperation,
22. Dependency Theory, 23. English, 24. France, 25. Civil Rights movement

MULTIPLE CHOICE:

1-c, 2-a, 3-d, 4-a, 5-b, 6-b, 7-d, 8-b, 9-c, 10-c, 11-a, 12-b, 13-a, 14-d, 15-d, 16-b, 17-b, 18-c, 19-a, 20-c, 21-a, 22-d, 23-b, 24-c, 25-b

MATCHING:

1-e, 2-j, 3-o, 4-a, 5-q, 6-s, 7-g, 8-p, 9-n, 10-i, 11-v, 12-x, 13-r, 14-d, 15-y, 16-m, 17-k, 18-u, 19-f, 20-w, 21-t, 22-b, 23-l, 24-h, 25-c

CHAPTER TWENTY-FOUR

A NEW EUROPE & THE TWENTY-FIRST CENTURY

IDENTIFICATION: Briefly describe each term.

Days of May

New Left

Richard Nixon

Détente

Soviet Economic Problems

Mikhail Gorbachev

Afghanistan War

perestroika

glasnost

Congress of People's Deputies

Andrei Sakharov

Lithuanian Supreme Council

Boris Yeltsin

Disintegration of the U.S.S.R.

Russian Free Market

Lech Walsea

John Paul II

Polish Catholic Church

Janos Kadar

Democratic Forum

Gustav Husak

Vaclav Havel

Nicolae Ceausescu

Todor Zhivkov

United Democratic Front

Erich Honecker

Stasi

Emigration

United Germany

Velvet Revolutions

Josip Tito

Slobodan Milosevic

Yugoslavian Wars

Ethnic Cleansing

Dayton Peace Settlement

Economic Recessions

European Community

Maastricht Treaty

Willy Brandt

Helmut Kohl

German Xenophobia

Irish Republican Army

British Coal Strike of 1984-1985

Nationality Act of 1982

Thatcherism

Reaganomics

Francois Mitterand

Jacques Chirac

Red Brigades

Democratic Party of the Left

Regionalist Leagues

Revolution of the Judges

Spanish Turn-Around

U.S. Relative Decline

Persian Gulf War

European Union

Group of 7

Global Environment

Jean-Jacques Servan-Schreiber

Green Parties

Global Warming

Simone de Beauvoir

Terrorism

September 11, 2001

Palestinian Terrorism

Militant Islamic Governments

Osama bin Laden

George W. Bush

Modernism

Pluralism

Post-Modernism

"Culture Wars"

TRUE/FALSE: Indicate whether each statement is true (T) or false (F). The correct answers are given at the end of the chapter.

_____1. The Soviet economy of the Brezhnev era prospered due to the efficiency of centralized planning.

_____2. The glasnost policy allowed Soviet citizens to discuss issues more freely.

_____3. In 1990 Lithuania became the first Soviet republic to declare independence.

_____4. The Soviet Union fell after losing a violent civil war.

_____5. The election of Pope John Paul II probably helped inspire the Polish people to demand more rights.

_____6. The Democratic Forum tried to restore Communism in Hungary.

_____7. Vaclav Havel became the first post-Communist president of Czechoslovakia.

_____8. Todor Zhivkov ran the Communist dictatorship of Bulgaria for 35 years.

_____9. Josip Tito led resistance against Communist rule in Yugoslavia.

_____10. The Dayton Peace Agreement endorsed the concept of ethnic cleansing.

_____11. The Maastricht Treaty formally recognized the reunification of Germany.

_____12. German xenophobia included resentment against recent immigrants.

_____13. The Nationality Act of 1982 permitted increased emigration from the U.S.S.R.

_____14. Francois Mitterand's socialist program in France nationalized key industries and raised living standards for the poor.

_____15. Italy's Communist Party renamed itself the "Democratic Party of the Left."

_____16. Spain saw rapid urbanization and urban growth through the 1970s.

_____17. The Common Market became the European Union and agreed on a standard currency.

_____18. Western and non-Western nations strongly agree on environmental issues.

_____19. Green Party candidates have been elected in several European countries.

_____20. Simone de Beauvoir was a leading figure in the Women's Liberation Movement.

_____21. All modern terrorism originates in the Middle East.

_____ 22. Palestinian terrorists have often received support from militant Islamic governments.

_____ 23. The Al-Qaeda organization was founded by Osama bin Laden.

_____ 24. According to the text, the most important recent Western cultural movement was the development of modernism.

_____ 25. "Culture Wars" are debates between Protestant and Catholic Christians.

FILL-IN-THE-BLANKS: Write the appropriate word(s) to complete the sentence. The correct answers are given at the end of the chapter.

1. _____rebelled against impersonalization and "technocracy" in Western society.

2. _____was the year of massive protest movements by youth in Europe and the United States

3. _____journeyed to China in 1972 and began the era of Détente.

4. _____ruled the Soviet Union under the slogan, "No experimentation."

5. _____recognized Eastern European borders in return for progress on human rights.

6. _____held the U.S. embassy staff hostage for 444 days.

7. _____is the Central Asian country where Soviet forces were defeated in a guerilla war.

8. _____was the Soviet leader whose reform efforts led to the fall of Communism.

9. _____was the first freely-elected Soviet legislature.

10. _____remained independent in Communist Poland and was the nucleus of resistance.

11. _____elected the United Democratic Front in 1991.

12. _____was the country whose Communist government was undermined by emigration.

13. _____is a term referring to revolutions in which Communist governments were replaced without much bloodshed.

14. _____was the first republic to declare independence from the Soviet Union.

15. _____was wracked by a series of vicious ethnic wars in the 1990s.

16. _____with "stagflation" struck Europe in 1973-1974 and 1979-1983.

17. _____has resorted to terrorism to contest British rule in Northern Ireland.

18. _____was a British economic and social policy that featured confrontation with unions, privatization of industries and housing, and deep cuts in social spending.

19. _____was the U. S. President who began a large military buildup and called the U.S.S.R. the "evil empire."

20. _____was elected President of France against an anti-Semitic extremist in 2001.

21. _____formed in Italian politics, as resentments grew between north and south.

22. _____suffered from "relative decline" after the Cold War ended.

23. _____replaced "Common Market."

24. _____moved to strengthen U. S. alliances to prosecute a war against terrorism.

25. _____is a movement that has resulted in less arrogance and greater questioning of cultural standards.

MULTIPLE CHOICE: Circle the correct response. The correct answers are given at the end of the chapter.

1. During the "Days of May" French students protested against all of the following except
    a. irrelevant curriculum
    b. environmental pollution
    c. bourgeois values
    d. authoritarian, bureaucratic administrators

2. The first leader to attempt to reconcile the Eastern and Western blocs in Europe was
   a. Mikhail Gorbachev
   b. Richard Nixon
   c. Leonid Brezhnev
   d. Willy Brandt

3. The Helsinki Agreement of 1975 called for
   a. the nonproliferation of nuclear weapons.
   b. the reunification of Eastern and Western Europe.
   c. respect for human rights in the Soviet bloc and the recognition of existing political boundaries.
   d. American de-escalation in Vietnam and Soviet withdrawal from Afghanistan.

4. Why did U.S. President Nixon's trip to China result in better relations with the Soviet Union?
   a. The Soviets made friends with any country that was on good terms with China.
   b. The Chinese agreed to send foreign aid to the Soviets.
   c. The U.S. agreed to withdraw from Vietnam.
   d. The Soviets feared the U.S. and China might ally against them.

5. What did Mikhail Gorbachev mean by perestroika?
   a. gradually allowing more private ownership and free enterprise into the Soviet economy.
   b. signing the ABM Treaty with the United States
   c. encouraging Soviet citizens to speak more openly
   d. permitting honest reporting of the news

6. What event prompted U. S. President Carter to impose economic sanctions on the Soviet Union and boycott the 1980 Summer Olympics?
   a. arrest of Andrei Sakharov
   b. violation of the SALT I Treaty
   c. invasion of Afghanistan
   d. Iranian hostage crisis

7. Overall, the reforms of Mikhail Gorbachev were intended to make the Soviet Union more
   a. repressive and violent
   b. free and decentralized
   c. militarily powerful
   d. resistant to change

8. How well did the new Russian free market economy perform?
   a. Russia enjoyed widespread growth and prosperity.
   b. There was little change from Communist days.
   c. A few got very wealthy, but overall the economy worsened.
   d. The free market economy performed so poorly that Communism was restored.

9. The election of laissez-faire advocates such as Margaret Thatcher in Britain and Ronald Reagan in the United States showed growing dissatisfaction with
   a. the military industrial complex
   b. capitalism
   c. the Cold War
   d. the social welfare state

10. Who led Poland's Solidarity Union Movement?
    a. John Paul II
    b. Lech Walsea
    c. Wladislaw Gomulka
    d. Wojciech Jaruzelski

11. Communism ended relatively peacefully in these countries except
    a. Hungary
    b. Czechoslovakia
    c. Romania
    d. Bulgaria

12. How did East Germans show their displeasure with Communist rule?
    a. Thousand fled the country when the opportunity arose.
    b. Resistance groups launched terrorist attacks.
    c. The citizens voted Erich Honecker out of power in 1989.
    d. Workers staged a nationwide strike that paralyzed the economy.

13. Which of the following was not an important factor in the collapse of Communist rule in Eastern Europe?
    a. Foreign aid from the United States and Western Europe
    b. Mikhail Gorbachev's announcement that the Soviet Army would no longer intervene to support Communist rulers
    c. The relative poverty of Eastern Europeans compared to Westerners
    d. The lack of civil liberties in Eastern Europe

14. Slobodan Milosevic ordered the Yugoslavian Army to invade all of the following <u>except</u>
    a. Bosnia
    b. Croatia
    c. Serbia
    d. Slovenia

15. The Maastricht Treaty was a move toward European unity in what two respects?
    a. government and defense
    b. economic and monetary
    c. economic and legal
    d. political and defense

16. What two groups faced discrimination in united Germany?
    a. Catholics and Jews
    b. Christians and Muslims
    c. Immigrants and East Germans
    d. Protestants and Social Democrats

17. Troubles in Northern Ireland stemmed from conflict between what two groups?
    a. Catholics and Protestants
    b. Communists and Socialists
    c. Northern and Southern Irish
    d. Irish and Republicans

18. To which British political party did Margaret Thatcher belong?
    a. Liberal Party
    b. Conservative Party
    c. Labour Party
    d. Whig Party

19. What was the effect of the British Nationality Act of 1982?
    a. It granted citizenship to all native-born nationalities.
    b. The Act excluded non-British nationalities from citizenship.
    c. It required all residents to swear allegiance to the British crown.
    d. The Act restricted nonwhite immigration from former colonies.

20. How did the economic ideas of Margaret Thatcher and Ronald Reagan differ from those of French President Francois Miterrand?
    a. Thatcher and Reagan increased aid to education while Miterrand cut it.
    b. Thatcher and Reagan increased social spending; Miterrand increased military spending.
    c. Thatcher and Reagan believed in strong government stimulation of the economy; Miterrand believed in privatization and laissez-faire.
    d. Thatcher and Reagan cut social spending and fought unions; Miterrand increased social spending and nationalized some industries.

21. To better serve their area's interests, Italian localities began to form
    a. Red Brigades
    b. Regionalist leagues
    c. Democratic Parties of the Left
    d. Provinces

22. What does the text mean by the "relative decline" of the United States?
    a. The United States is no longer the most powerful nation in the world.
    b. The U.S. is still the most powerful, but not by as great a margin as before.
    c. The U.S. is losing its might and will probably fall soon.
    d. The U.S. will stop declining and soon become more powerful than ever.

23. Describe Spain's recent economic performance.
    a. Spain has modernized and urbanized to a great extent.
    b. Spain continues to lag behind the rest of Europe.
    c. Spain's economy is now the strongest in Europe.
    d. Spain, like Russia, is trying to adjust from Communism to a free market.

24. What motivated the terrorist attacks of Osama bin Laden and his Al-Qaeda organization?
    a. hatred of Christianity and a desire to eradicate it
    b. a desire to bring Communism to the Middle East
    c. resentment against Western influence in Muslim countries
    d. hatred against democracy

25. Modernism is concerned with the drive to
    a. build a modern industrial state
    b. spread democracy throughout the world
    c. reevaluate all values
    d. apply the lessons of science to all aspects of modern life

MATCHING: Match the response in column B with the item in column A.

Column A

_____ 1. Group formed to control oil pricing and production.

_____ 2. Richard Nixon's policy of easing tensions with Communist powers.

_____ 3. Proposals to decentralize the Soviet economic system.

_____ 4. Soviet scientist, dissident, and finally legislator.

_____ 5. First president of the Russian Federation.

_____ 6. Leader of Solidarity movement and later president of Poland.

_____ 7. Reforming Communist leader of Hungary.

_____ 8. Repressive Communist leader of Czechoslovakia.

_____ 9. Brutal Communist dictator of Romania.

_____ 10. Tyrannical Communist leader of East Germany.

_____ 11. Reunified officially on October 3, 1990.

_____ 12. Genocidal Serbian leader of Yugoslavia.

_____ 13. It divided Bosnia into Muslim, Croat, and Serbian areas.

_____ 14. First chancellor of united Germany.

_____ 15. Leader who defeated the coal miner's strike of 1984-1985.

_____ 16. U.S. policy to sharply cut taxes and social welfare spending.

_____ 17. Italian terrorist group active in the late 1970s.

_____ 18. Movement to clean up Italian political corruption.

_____ 19. Conflict in which a U.S.-led coalition drove Iraq out of Kuwait.

_____ 20. "Executive Committee" of the world's economy.

_____ 21. He warned against Europe becoming subservient to the United States.

_____ 22. Environmental change caused by burning fossil fuel and destroying rain forests.

_____ 23. Destroyed by the terrorist attacks of September 11, 2001.

_____ 24. Iran, Iraq, Syria, and Libya

_____ 25. Movement that believes meaning is only imparted by the reader of a text.

Column B

a. Germany
c. Boris Yeltsin
e. Détente
g. Global warming
i. Erich Honecker
k. OPEC
m. Andrei Sakharov
o. Margaret Thatcher
q. Lech Walsea
s. Gustav Husak
u. Dayton Peace Agreement
w. Jean-Jacques Servan-Schreiber
y. Nicolae Ceacescu

b. Helmut Kohl
d. Post-modernism
f. Revolution of the judges
h. Perestroika
j. Militant Islamic governments
l. Janos Kadar
n. Group of 7
p. World Trade Center
r. Slobodan Milosevic
t. Red Brigades
v. Reaganomics
x. Persian Gulf War

ESSAY QUESTIONS: (Answer on separate paper)

1. In what ways has Europe integrated as a region? Do you believe there will one day be a "United States of Europe?" Why or why not?

2. Describe the fall of Communism in Eastern Europe or the Soviet Union. What factors were most important in leading to this major historical development?

3. Evaluate Pluralism and Postmodernism and their roles in contemporary Western Civilization.

ANSWERS TO CHAPTER TWENTY-FOUR

TRUE/FALSE:

1-F; 2-T; 3-T; 4-F; 5-T; 6-F; 7-T; 8-T; 9-F; 10-F; 11-F; 12-T; 13-F; 14-T; 15-T; 16-T; 17-T; 18-F; 19-T; 20-T; 21-F; 22-T; 23-T; 24-T; 25-F

FILL-IN-THE-BLANKS:

1. The New Left 2. 1968 3. Richard Nixon 4. Leonid Brezhnev 5. Helsinki Agreement 6. Iran 7. Afghanistan 8. Mikhail Gorbachev 9. Congress of People's Deputies 10. Polish Catholic Church 11. Bulgaria 12. East Germany 13. Velvet Revolutions 14. Lithuania 15. Yugoslavia 16. Economic recessions 17. Irish Republican Army 18. Thatcherism 19. Ronald Reagan 20. Jacques Chirac 21. Regionalist Leagues 22. The United States 23. European Community 24. George W. Bush 25. Pluralism

MULTIPLE CHOICE:

1-b; 2-d; 3-c; 4-d; 5-a; 6-c; 7-b; 8-c; 9-d; 10-b; 11-c; 12-a; 13-a; 14-c; 15-b; 16-c; 17-a; 18-b; 19-d; 20-d; 21-b; 22-b; 23-a; 24-c; 25-c

MATCHING:

1-k; 2-e; 3-h; 4-m; 5-c; 6-q; 7-l; 8-s; 9-y; 10-i; 11-a; 12-r; 13-u; 14-b; 15-o; 16-v; 17-t; 18-f; 19-x; 20-n; 21-w; 22-g; 23-p; 24-j; 25-d

Notes

Notes

Notes

Notes

Notes

Notes